# HARDY PALMS
## AND
# PALM-LIKE PLANTS

## MARTYN GRAHAM

GUILD OF MASTER CRAFTSMAN PUBLICATIONS

With thanks to my mother, for her infinite patience in typing the original manuscript, and to Martin Gibbons for his valued support in encouraging me to write about palms. Special thanks to Nigel Kent Hutchings for his invaluable advice regarding the photography.

First published 2002 by Guild of Master Craftsman Publications Ltd, 166 High Street, Lewes, East Sussex, BN7 1XU

Copyright in the Work © Guild of Master Craftsman Publications Ltd
Text copyright © Martyn Graham
Maps © Carrie Hill

ISBN 1 86108 267 3
A catalogue record of this book is available from the British Library
Photographs by Martyn Graham except:
Martin Gibbons and Tobias W. Spanner pp95,102,106,107,108;
Nigel Kent Hutchings pp7(both),47,55(top pair),56(top pair),58(top),
65,66,110,112(bottom); Harry Smith Collection p134

Designed by Christopher Halls at Mind's Eye Design, Lewes

Colour origination by Universal Graphics (Singapore)
Printed in Singapore by Kyodo

# CONTENTS

# PREFACE

When I became interested in palms some 25 years ago the available selection was limited to the humble Parlour palm and, if you were lucky, the odd Chusan palm (*Trachycarpus fortunei*) lying neglected in a forgotten corner of the local garden centre. How things have changed! These days 15 or 20 species are routinely available, Chusan palms are a common sight in suburban gardens and you can buy unusual palms not only in the garden centre, but in the florist and even in the greengrocers. Specialist nurseries are springing up all over the place to accommodate this explosion in interest, and along with it there is a hunger for information on which species to grow, how to grow them and where to find them.

In his new book Martyn Graham, long-time customer at The Palm Centre, has committed his wide experience of these matters to paper, describing those species of palms and other exotic plants he considers most suitable for our climate, how to look after them and how to protect them. Excellent photographs accompany the text, and a Plant Directory provides a readily accessible and wide-ranging catalogue of suitable plants from which to choose.

I wish Martyn and all those who read this book good luck and much pleasure in following this rewarding and fascinating hobby.

Martin Gibbons
The Palm Centre
August 2002

# INTRODUCTION

There are few plants that epitomize the exotic and tropical more than palm trees and their cousins the spiky plants. Their silhouettes are distinctive – instantly recognizable – and have a great impact in temperate climates because they are not often associated with these regions. In fact, there are over 100 species that will flourish in temperate regions and it is unlikely that there won't be a plant suitable for your garden, whatever its soil type or the amount of shade.

Increasingly, people view their gardens as outdoor rooms and as such, wish to create and decorate them with style. You can incorporate a sense of the exotic by degree, according to your preference. In Chapter 8 I have listed complementary plants that could be used to create a planter, a bed or a whole garden following a jungle, Mediterranean or exotic theme.

All the species listed in the Directory are suitable for growing in a temperate garden, though how well individual plants fare will depend upon your understanding of the local climate and of the microclimates existing in your garden. Armed with the necessary information, you can assess which plants are most appropriate for you.

On the other side of the Atlantic, in the pre-Columbian Americas, agaves were fermented to produce alcoholic drinks, while in New Zealand, cordyline hearts have been cooked, producing a cabbage-like food, for millennia.

Today, palms and palm-like plants are fashionable in many countries. They first caught the Western imagination when the Victorians, great explorers, brought back many species from distant shores. It is thanks to plant hunters such as Robert Fortune that there are 150-year-old examples of the Chusan palm growing in England; some specimens are now over 15m (45ft) tall.

For much of the nineteenth century the tropical look was in vogue and this gave plant hunters the financial impetus to continue their search. Today, with fashion again creating a strong demand, specialist nurseries can even supply specimens many metres high and weighing tons. At the other end of the scale, a wide range of seeds is available at very modest prices. However, you need to be patient with seeds as it may take a decade to grow a sizeable plant.

If you want to grow palms, you must be realistic about how much time you have to tend your garden. If it isn't a lot, choose those plants that will cope best with neglect. Yuccas generally need only modest watering, usually less than palms as there are few true desert palms. In fact, many palms are forest understorey plants where damp conditions are the norm.

SECTION ONE

# GROWTH AND MAINTENANCE

APPEARANCE AND CULTURAL REQUIREMENTS

REQUIREMENTS

MICROCLIMATES

MAINTENANCE

PROPAGATION

BUYING SPECIMEN PLANTS

# CHAPTER ONE

# APPEARANCE AND CULTURAL REQUIREMENTS

**W**hile the growth habits of palms vary from one species to another, there are some habits that can be attributed to palms and palm-like plants generally, giving them, as a group, a common appearance.

## APPEARANCE

### Stems

While the majority of palms have a single trunk, some, such as *Chamaedorea microspadix*, are multiple-stemmed and suckering by nature. Some species can produce both single- and multi-stemmed plants.

### Leaves

Although palms are usually green, there are also blue (e.g. *Brahea armata*) and variegated types (e.g. *Rhapis excelsa*). Few palms can match the sumptuous sky-blue leaves of *Brahea armata*. Even the green of different palms varies from deep to lime. The spiky plants also exhibit varying shades of green but it is the range of variegated yellow, blue and red leaves they offer that makes them so useful in a garden.

Palms have four leaf types. Most that will grow in a temperate climate are mainly fan (palmate) or feather (pinnate) in shape, although a few are fishtail. *Trachycarpus fortunei* leaves can grow to over 1m (3ft 3in) in length whereas those of *Chamaerops humilis* rarely reach more than 40cm (1ft 3in). In colder climates, the leaves of many spiky plants will become thicker and stiffer in order to cope with frosts; in hot climates, the leaves remain thinner as this allows them to lose heat more quickly.

If you have young children it is worth avoiding sharp plants like many of the yuccas and agaves; the soft leaves found in cordylines and phormiums will offer a safer choice.

The yellow and green leaves of a rare *Trachycarpus fortunei*

*Trithrinax campestris* has the sharpest leaves of any temperate climate palms

## Palmate

The number of lealets in the fan increases as the tree gets older. The individual leaflet ends may be flat or pointed, according to the species.

The fan-shaped leaves of *Trachycarpus fortunei* make an excellent architectural feature

### Feather-shaped

Pinnate palms have a central stem to which the leaflets are attached, like a feather. Some are evenly distributed in one plane, others grow in alternate directional planes. Caryota palms have an unusual variation – their leaves resemble fish tails.

The pinnate leaf of a *Phoenix canariensis*

## SPECIES OF NOTE

The leaves of *Butia capitata* look extremely exotic which is not surprising as it is a native of south Brazil. To me they are like sculpted jade. Cheaper, and with a different-looking leaf, is *Phoenix canariensis*. This versatile palm can be grown in both temperate and dry tropical climates. The avenues of palms in Spain are invariably planted with this species. *Phoenix theophrasti* has a distinctly different leaf from *P. canariensis* and makes an excellent specimen plant, though its growing apex needs protection in frosty conditions.

While more expensive than the palms above, *Jubaea chilensis* has a fantastic leaf shape and, in time, forms a majestic trunk. Its slow rate of growth makes it suitable for long-term pot culture, though it is reputed to grow noticeably faster in the ground.

Rows of Washingtonias are an impressive sight

# Flowers

Although people don't often think of palms as spectacular flowering trees, they can be. The *Trachycarpus fortunei* palm in my front garden has 1m (3ft) long bracts smothered with yellow flowers and the flowering period can last anything up to a month. I've seen as many as eight bracts clothing the top of the palm in early summer and more than one passer-by has commented on its beauty.

Yuccas have amazing spires of creamy flowers that rise from the middle of the plant. Depending upon the species and the size of the individual plant, they can reach up to 5m (16ft 6in) in height. The flowering period, determined to some extent by weather conditions, can last several months. The flower spires on

*Astelia chathamica* 'Silver Spear' just coming into flower

The spires of a flowering *Yucca gloriosa*

phormiums can reach over 2m (6ft 6in), but their orange flowers tend to be less showy. The bracts of cordylines carry eye-catching creamy flowers for several weeks of the year and the flowering spikes of agaves can grow many metres higher than the plant.

A profusion of flowering bracts

The long and resplendent spire of a flowering yucca

*W. filifera* in flower (left) with *Washingtonia robusta*

# Seeds and fruit

After flowering a female palm will form seeds if the tree has
a specimen of the opposite sex growing nearby to enable
pollination. Some species are self-pollinating and will form
fertile seeds on their own. Ripe seeds vary in colour from black,
through brown and yellow, to red. Even though they are not
showy they can brighten up an autumn day.

The dark seed pods of a yucca

Palm fruits add a band of colour

A dense growth of red berries on a *Chamaerops humilis*

Though most of the plants listed in the Directory don't bear edible fruits, some do. In Brazil, the fruits of palms such as *Butia capitata* are used to make both jelly and wine, while in Chile the sap of *Jubaea chilensis* is used to make wine as well as a delicious honey. In the past trees had to be killed in order to extract the sap but new methods allow it to be bled off periodically without any harm to the plant.

# GROWTH RATE

If you are using palms in a mixed planting of herbaceous plants, shrubs and trees, you must allow for their speed of growth and final height: unlike shrubs, palms can rarely be cut back to control their size. Generally, plants originating from a cool

Some large palms, such as this *Trachycarpus fortunei*, can easily dominate a front garden

In hotter climates, the trunks of *Trachycarpus fortunei* grow fast and stay thin

climate will grow faster than those from warmer regions. For example, a *Trachycarpus fortunei* with a 1m (3ft) trunk can grow in excess of 30cm (1ft) a year if it has acclimatized to a temperate climate. However, desert palms such as Braheas might grow only 1cm (⅜in) a year. Slow-growing palms are excellent for pots, which is useful in situations where space is limited, as on a terrace roof garden.

In 2000, research carried out at Miami's Fairchild Tropical Garden showed an average annual growth of 15.5cm (6in). The average age of the trees was 30.6 years. What was especially interesting was the range of growth rates – between 2 and 54cm (⅞ and 21in). So, if you grow a variety of palms, their growth rates could vary greatly. It may take a palm trunk centuries to reach its full height in a temperate climate.

Hardiness zones are allocated according to average minimum winter temperatures of an area (see maps pp 163–165). Up to a certain temperature, heat will stimulate palms to grow faster but above this, palms originating from a temperate region will grow increasingly poorly the hotter it gets. Even in the comparatively mild climate of a zone 8 region, the degree of summer heat will have an effect on a plant's rate of growth.

The rate of growth of agaves varies according to the species. *Agave americana* is very popular because of its rapid growth rate; young plants can double in size within a year. Most other agaves are much slower growing.

Cycads grow slowly but do have spurts of growth related to their sexual cycle. In mature plants, male and female flowers are formed during these spurts.

Younger palms tend to grow faster than mature ones, although they can take several years to settle in. Some yuccas double in size within two years while others are much slower, and while cordylines can take 10 years to form a 1m (3ft) trunk, they can double in size within a year before they form one. Phormiums often double in size each year so that within five years a small plant will have formed a clump with dozens of leaves.

Where you live will radically affect your plants' growth rates because of differences in such things as hours and intensity of sunlight, the average cloud cover and the degree of heat during the active growing period. The trunk of a *Washingtonia filifera* in south-east France, just within a zone 8 region (winter lows of -10°C [14°F] were recorded), grew from 50cm to 4m (1ft 4in to 13ft) within a decade. The trunk of a *Phoenix canariensis* in the same area grew from 50cm to 2m (1ft 4in to 6ft 6in) during the same period. Around London, also within a zone 8 region, a growth rate one-third of that would be considered a success, while in central Scotland you might only achieve one-third of the London rate.

## Cloches

A technique popular with some palm enthusiasts is to surround a small plant with a cloche for several years. The results of this technique obviously vary according to how sunny your local climate is, but growth rates can be significantly increased.

However, palms that rarely experience temperatures above 25°C (77°F) in their native environment (for example, *Parajubaea torallyi*) must not be overheated as excessive heat can be detrimental to their growth. For species such as these, the use of cloches outside summer may help optimize growth, but they should not be used during the hottest months.

## TYPICAL GROWTH PATTERNS

Palms can be classified into three growing groups, though individual plants can move from one group to another as they mature.

Cold-hardy and grow well *Trachycarpus* spp., *Chamaerops*, *Butia* spp. and *Jubaea*.

Cold-hardy but slow-growing *Rhapidophyllum hystrix*, *Nannorrhops ritchiana*, *Sabal minor* and *Trithrinax campestris*

Need protection against low temperatures but good growers in cool summers *Washingtonia* spp., *Ceroxylon* spp., *Arenga engleri* and *Rhopalostylis* spp.

## Lifespan

Generally, the slower growing a plant, the longer it will live. This is because a tree can only grow to a certain height: the pressure required for water and nutrients to reach the topmost leaves can be met only up to a certain point, and as the trunk grows, the leaves are having to provide for an increasingly hungry tree. The life expectancy of many of the plants in the Directory exceeds the average life expectancy for humans. Because plants grow at a slower rate in a temperate climate, they should live much longer under such conditions.

The oldest botanical garden in the world, Orto Botanico Di Padova in Padua, Italy, was planted out in 1585 and you can still see many of the original plants there today. A *Livistona eastonii* in Australia is estimated to be 700 years old. It appears that, as long as palms do not succumb to changing climatic conditions, they can live for centuries.

Many spiky plants also have long lives. I know of an agave that is about 100 years old which is just starting to flower – they don't call it the century plant for nothing.

# CHAPTER TWO

# REQUIREMENTS

An understanding of the requirements of plants will enable you to identify the best locations for individual species, and correct siting will allow you to grow the widest possible range of plants.

## SOIL

Most palms aren't fussy about the pH value of the soil they grow in but there are a few exceptions worth noting: *Trachycarpus martianus*, *Caryota hymalayana* and *Ceroxylon* spp. especially, all need an acid soil to do well. You can raise the acidity of the soil by adding sequestrenes to it. This will also help prevent chlorosis (yellowing of the leaves caused by a lack of iron) as sequestrenes contain iron.

A good general planting mix would have a ratio of two parts organic material to three parts soil and one part sand, with a slow-release fertilizer. You can alter this mix radically to help borderline plants, especially those from dry areas. In this case grit and sand could easily form 50 per cent of the mix, as this will help water to drain away more quickly, and plants from dry areas dislike cold, damp soils. Plants originating from a forest location prefer a high organic content in their planting mix.

## Organic matter

Adding organic matter to any soil will darken its colour and this, in turn, will cause it to absorb more heat from the sun and warm up more quickly. When applied as a mulch, it helps to insulate the soil and keep it from freezing in the winter. An organic mulch will also trap water beneath it. While this is desirable in dry periods, you must be careful not to put too much mulch next to the stem of a plant in hot, wet weather as this may cause the stem to rot.

# WATER

Plants originating from areas with desert conditions require significantly less watering than those from a forest or temperate region; a desert palm may need only one-quarter of the water required by a plant of similar size from a temperate region. Collapsing leaves and splits appearing in the trunk indicate that a plant is being overwatered. All palms and spiky plants prefer to be kept on the dry side during the winter: excessively wet and cold roots may rot, and frozen water, along with the nutrients it contains, cannot be absorbed by the roots. Ensuring that the roots are kept dry in winter will allow the widest range of plants to be grown. I have found that leaving the roots of plants in pots to dry out before watering them again will produce the healthiest plants.

If you have to plant in a wet area, it may be worth placing the plant on the ground and mounding soil around it rather than digging a hole to plant it in. Where the ground is very waterlogged, you may need to introduce land drains to take away excessive water. In dry areas you should apply mulches routinely in order to help conserve water, and where water shortages are a serious problem, push tubes into the root areas to funnel water directly to them.

# FROST PROTECTION

All cycads and the more sensitive spiky plants require frost protection. Generally, the younger a palm, no matter how hardy it is as a mature specimen, the greater protection it will need. As a rule, it is not worth planting a palm outside unless its roots fill a 15cm (6in) pot and it has reached at least 30cm (1ft) in height – with palms, patience always pays. The width of the trunk can also contribute to a plant's frost-hardiness; in order for *Washingtonia filifera* to have a hardiness of down to -9°C (-16°F), you must use a wide-trunked specimen. However, by utilizing the advice given in Chapter 3 regarding the use of microclimates and planting conditions, a surprising range of plants can be grown in a temperate climate.

When you consider a plant's hardiness to the cold, it is best to think of it in terms of a process. Depending upon the original size of the plant and its natural hardiness, it could take between 5 and 25 years for it to approach its maximum hardiness. For example, a five-year-old *Trachycarpus fortunei* palm would reach a high percentage of its potential hardiness within five years if it was well looked after, however, a marginal palm such as *Rhopalostylis sapida* takes 25 years of growth just to cope with occasional lows of -5°C (23°F).

The beautiful pinnate leaves of *Rhopalostylis sapida*

So why grow *R. sapida* in a temperate climate? First, it has a uniquely attractive foliage. Second, it copes with considerable shade, especially when young. Third, it grows at a reasonable speed in cool conditions. It is frost rather than low temperatures that causes the most damage to palms; by overwintering a rhopalostylis palm in a greenhouse with heating just enough to keep the frost at bay, you should be able to grow a good specimen.

The degree of frost a palm is subjected to and how long the frost lasts are both crucial factors. If snow settles heavily on a plant's leaves, especially large fan leaves, it may be worth gently shaking it off to keep the leaves from snapping, though in areas with heavy falls, hardy plants may

*Rhopalostylis sapida* can reach a good height even in cool conditions

benefit from the insulating qualities of the snow. A layer of snow can make a difference of 10°C (18°F) – which can mean the difference between life and death for many plants in particularly low temperatures. In addition, research into hardiness at Ohio University showed that snow-covered palms frequently protected smaller specimens during prolonged periods of harsh weather and a wide selection of palms was shown to have much higher hardiness ratings than previously thought. This was especially true when even simple protection was provided in freezing conditions.

In the USA, growing the plants listed in this book in weather conditions below zone 8 will require the maximum use of overwintering techniques. Though the hot summer conditions experienced in some cold winter areas will help to produce strong and healthy plants, it would be best to stick with the most cold-hardy plants when they are to be subjected to low winter temperatures.

It must also be remembered that keeping roots dry in freezing weather benefits all plants: nutrients cannot be absorbed when the roots are frozen as they are carried in water. For agaves, dry roots are essential: if their roots are not adequately protected from frost, their leaves will blacken and shrink back to the growing centre. While a number can be hardy to -20°C (-4°F), they would need bone-dry conditions to achieve this.

The smaller a plant, the more protection it will need in its formative years. Plants that were grown in a warmer environment (in a different location or in a greenhouse) benefit from protection, even when large and mature, when they are planted out in a new environment. I have seen sizeable plants ruined due to this lack of initial protection, while a plant of the same species, half the size but properly hardened off, remained untouched in my garden.

Because some plants come from regions that enjoy hot summers, they often grow very slowly in cooler, temperate areas. Palms such as Sabals just cope within zone 8 areas in the south of England but would not be worth growing in most of Scotland. Certain palms grow better in the hot, continental summers of much of the USA than in maritime zone 8 regions. Understanding your climate and what will grow well in it is essential if you want your plants to reach their full potential. (See p 159 for details of palm societies whose local members are usually only too pleased to offer advice on the best plants to grow. Reputable nurseries should also be useful sources of information.)

# PLANTS FOR THE COLDEST REGIONS

| PALMS | DEGREES C/F |
|---|---|
| Trachycarpus fortunei | -18/0 |
| Trachycarpus takil | -19/2 |
| Trachycarpus wagnerianus | -19/2 |
| Nannorrhops ritchiana (needs hot summers) | -18/0 |
| Sabal minor (needs hot summers) | -18/0 |
| Rhapidophyllum hystrix (needs hot summers) | -18/0 |
| Jubaea chilensis | -12/10 |
| Butia capitata | -12/10 |
| Phoenix canariensis | -10/14 |
| Phoenix theophrasti | -11/12 |
| Chamaedorea radicalis | -10/14 |
| Chamaedorea microspadix | -10/14 |

| CORDYLINES | |
|---|---|
| C. indivisa (green) | -10/14 |
| C. australis (green) | -12/10 |
| Green | -12/10 |
| Purple | -9/16 |
| Other colours | -8/17 and lower |

| YUCCAS | |
|---|---|
| Y. glauca | -37/-35 |
| Y. filamentosa | -29/-20 |
| Y. flaccida | -29/-20 |
| Y. pallida | -18/0 |
| Y. rostrata | -15/5 |

| AGAVES | |
|---|---|
| A. parryi | -29/-20 |
| A. harrimaniae var. neomexicana | -29/-20 |
| A. utahensis | -23/-9 |
| A. havardiana | -23/-9 |

| CYCADS | |
|---|---|
| Cycas panzhihuaensis | -8/17 |
| Cycas revoluta | -6/21 |

NB  Temperatures refer to mature hardened-off plants. Small and unhardened-off specimens may cope with only one-third of the temperatues in the above table.

# CHAPTER THREE

# MICROCLIMATES

Once you have identified your general climate and which plants will grow happily in it, you must evaluate the microclimates that exist within your garden. The exploitation of these, and the correct location of plants in your garden, will allow you to grow the widest possible range and to keep them in their best condition.

## WIND

Winds can make or break a plant. During the winter their drying effect can cause water to be lost at a faster rate than it can be absorbed, and if the ground is frozen the roots won't be able to take up water, so the drying wind will cause plants to wilt. There is also the wind-chill factor (which will, in effect, reduce the ambient temperature) to consider.

So what can be done to reduce the damaging effects of wind? If you live in a windy location it is best to grow plants with short, stiff leaves as they are less likely to be shredded by wind than longer, softer varieties. *Trachycarpus wagnerianus* would be a good choice whereas the leaves of *T. fortunei* can shred very easily in exposed sites. Avoid placing your most tender plants and those with the largest leaves to face the prevailing winds. Select your hardiest plants and those with linear leaves for such locations: linear leaves tend to be more flexible than broader leaves and also catch the wind less. A stiff-leaved yucca will cope with these conditions much better than a fan palm.

Short, stiff *Trachycarpus Wagnerianus* leaves such as these are a good choice for a windy position

Secondly, cultivate a screen of shrubs or trees to diffuse winds and reduce any turbulence. Alternatively, put up a non-solid fence such as a picket fence. When wind strikes a solid screen or wall, it is forced up and over it to hit the ground on the other side, where damaging eddies can shred leaves and break branches. The resultant movement of the tree also loosens its roots; this may not cause the plant to topple but it does create spaces around the roots in which water can puddle and freeze.

The longer leaves of *Trachycarpus fortunei* are susceptible to wind damage

In addition, a solid screen at the bottom of a hill will trap frost at its base – being denser than warm air, cold air will drop to the bottom of a valley or slope – causing unnecessary harm to any plants there. A wall of plants will reduce this problem as any air pockets can filter through.

Windbreaks by the sea have the added advantage of reducing the salt content of the wind – salt can all too easily burn foliage. If you are planting a coastal windbreak, always choose salt-tolerant plants such as escallonia.

# SOIL

You need to assess what soil type you have, how free-draining it is, and what organic content it has as these factors determine which species you can grow.

## Sandy soils

Sandy soil is free-draining, due to its large particle size, and quick to dry. This is good news in the winter, as water is less likely to freeze, but bad in the summer, when water evaporates more rapidly and may be scarce. However, you can increase its water-holding capacity by adding organic matter and the coarser the better, as coarser matter will be broken down more slowly by this hungry soil. As sandy soil tends to be alkaline, the acidic compost will help neutralize the soil.

## Clay soils

Clay soils are probably the hardest to get into good condition though in their favour, they do have a high nutrient content. In the winter the small mineral particles in them stick together and impede good drainage while in hot summer weather they form a rock-hard pan that is even harder to work than sticky wet clay. You can create a much better soil by applying copious amounts of compost and grit or sand, and you can help to reduce stickiness and lower acidity by adding hydrated lime.

## Chalky soils

Chalky soils are free-draining but break down organic matter quickly so they need annual mulches to keep them in top condition. While chalky soils are alkaline, you can add sulphate of iron to help make them more neutral.

# FROST

There are a number of factors that affect how hardy a plant is to frost. These, the first six of which are discussed in previous chapters, are listed below:

- the age of the plant
- the local humidity
- the drainage rate of the soil
- exposure to sun
- the prevailing winds
- acclimatization to local conditions
- the degree of protection provided in winter

The black marks on this leaf are the result of frost damage when the leaf was emerging in an earlier winter

23

Encasing plants in straw or moving them to a warmer location should allow most of the plants listed in the Directory to survive harsh winters without problems. Siting next to a sunny wall, especially that of a house, will allow heat to radiate from the bricks to the plant during the night; the plant will also benefit if the house is centrally heated during the winter. Planting next to evergreen trees and shrubs, which offer considerable protection from cold weather, is another means of modifying the local climate.

An insulating layer of straw, held in place with horticultural fleece

It is easy to wrap horticultural fleece or hessian around a palm in frosty weather to protect it from modest frost levels. Bubble wrap can also be used, but it should not be left on for too long as it will encourage the growth of fungi between it and the palm. Rope the fronds of larger palms together before wrapping fleece or hessian around them. For particularly large palms, seek help from a couple of assistants to make the job easier. The leaves of cordylines and phormiums are easy to pull together and secure, but yucca leaves are stiffer and need the protection of a straw stuffing between them as well as a covering of fleece. In major frost areas, greater protection can be achieved by placing a thick layer of hay within a mesh screen.

The most critical part of a palm is its growing apex and this can be well stuffed with hay. Attaching a waterproof covering, such as a sheet of plastic, above the apex in cold weather will stop excessive amounts of water freezing around this area.

Spray your plants with an insecticide or fungicide before wrapping them up for the winter. Spraying the growing centre of borderline hardy palms can help prevent them from rotting.

To increase the hardiness of the plant, remove all forms of protection when no frost is expected.

The leaves of *Cordyline australis* tied together to guard against frost damage

In particularly harsh weather, cover your plants with an extra layer of fleece for added protection

# CHAPTER FOUR

# MAINTENANCE

As with any living thing, palms need food and water in order to grow and remain healthy. Regular pruning can also help keep a plant looking as good as possible.

## WATERING

During the growing season, regular watering will help maximize the speed of growth of a palm. In dry conditions a policy of heavy watering several times a week will help the tree develop deeper root systems than a light daily watering: with light watering, the moisture will not soak deeply into the soil, so there is no reason for the roots to grow, but less frequent, heavier watering will require the roots to penetrate more deeply in order to find the water. How much water to apply depends upon the size of the plant; a *Trachycarpus fortunei* with a 2m (6ft 6in) trunk could have a hose left on its base for 5 minutes twice a week.

During the winter, indoor and conservatory plants require watering only once every few weeks but they may benefit from being sprayed with water, especially if your house is centrally heated. This is particularly true for plants that originate from jungles, such as Chamaedoreas, as they dislike the excessively dry conditions created by this.

Summer watering depends upon the size of the plant and the temperatures experienced, but it is better to water heavily and let the plant dry out between waterings rather than water a little each day.

# FERTILIZING

## Palms

Use fertilizers that contain adequate amounts of nitrogen, phosphorus, potassium and magnesium, if possible in the ratio of 3:1:3:1. Although it has equal amounts of the first three components, I usually use National Growmore because it is cheap and readily available. You might need to add trace elements such as magnesium occasionally. These are usually sold in powder form. The condition of the leaves will indicate deficiencies and excesses of trace elements, as listed:

- magnesium deficiency – yellowing of the outer leaves
- iron deficiency – yellowing of all the leaves, sometimes accompanied by the development of green spots
- zinc deficiency – stunted leaves and die-back in new leaves
- zinc excess – yellowing and spotting of leaves
- copper deficiency – stunting in new leaves
- boron deficiency – stunting and crumbling in new leaves
- molybdenum deficiency – yellowing of leaves and browning in leaf tips
- nitrogen deficiency – yellowing of leaves

Start fertilizing in the spring, once the cold weather has finished. It is best for the nitrogen to be absorbed by the next frosts to reduce the chance of soft growth being burnt back; stop granular fertilizing by mid-summer and liquid fertilizing by late summer so that when the first frosts occur, most of the nitrogen has been absorbed and is no longer creating soft new growth. In the early autumn, a foliar feed of potassium can help harden off your palm for the winter. A mature, fast-growing palm in my garden (in suburban London) can absorb ½kg (1lb) of ferilizer each month between early spring and late summer. The slower the likely growth of a palm, whether due to its species or the coolness of the climate, the less fertilizer it will need. A Brahea would only need 30 per cent of the fertilizer used by a *Trachycarpus fortunei*.

## Cordylines

Cordylines have the same requirements as temperate palms.

## Yuccas

Yuccas require only light fertilizing; around one-quarter of what you would feed a palm of similar size.

## Phormiums and astelias

A general fertilizer can be applied during the growing season. As these plants have no stem, you must take care not to let the fertilizer lie on the centre of the plant where it may burn the foliage; place it around the base of the plant to avoid this.

## Agaves

I recommend only light fertilizing. As agave leaves store water for the plant, they are naturally quite soft. Nitrogen has the effect of further softening the outer parts of the leaf, which leaves them more susceptible to damage from frosts.

## Cycads

Cycads have similar requirements to palms but as they don't grow quickly, slow-release fertilizers tend to be the best option. These can be supplemented with liquid fertilizers when there is a period of strong growth and new fronds.

# PESTS AND DISEASES

Pests and diseases are rarely a problem for palms and palm-like plants growing outside, especially in temperate climates. This is partly due to the fact that leaves tend to be harder in cold environments, which makes it more difficult for sap-sucking insects to penetrate them. However, fungus can be a problem if the plant is in a damp, shady site in which the leaves take some time to dry off.

In hotter climates, palms are more common with the result that diseases carried by insects can spread quickly in a particular area, where such plants may be found in every other garden.

The fungus on this phormium leaf was encouraged by shade and the poor circulation of air around the plant

## Indoor plants

Generally, indoor plants don't need heavy feeding so slow-release fertilizers are the best: without direct sun they grow more slowly and so require less food. Over many years, salts can build up in the compost so a thorough drenching to leach them out, once every three years, would be beneficial.

# PRUNING

Generally, the leaves of the plants listed in the Directory should only be removed when they are dead. However, you could make an exception for such palms as *Trachycarpus fortunei*. Their leaves can remain on the trunk until they reach ground level, but they are often removed from the lower branches of mature specimens, for appearance's sake. Usually, at least half of the bottom leaves are pruned though many people prefer to remove at least two-thirds.

Never cut the head off a single-trunk palm as this will prevent it from ever generating new leaves and, in time, will cause it to die. You can remove excess and older canes of multi-stemmed palms periodically. After flowering, bracts can be cut a few centimetres away from the trunk. Old leaves should also be cut a few centimetres from the trunk.

Damaged agaves are best pruned when their foliage has dried out and become shrivelled. Yuccas and cordylines also need their old leaves removed. For these plants, and for phormiums, if old leaves do not pull away easily, use sharp shears to cut them off. Remove spent flower spikes by cutting as far down their spike as possible; secateurs are usually the best tool for this job.

Use sharp secateurs to remove dead leaves (above) and flower spikes (below)

# INDOOR PESTS

Although the plants listed in the Directory are rarely bothered by insects when planted in the garden, when they are grown indoors they can be affected. Aphids and red spider mites can both be a problem. One approach is to spray plants with an insecticide as soon as you see the insects. Another is to introduce natural insect predators to control the pests – small parasitic wasps can be bought from garden suppliers, and these help to keep insect numbers down.

# CHAPTER FIVE

# PROPAGATION

The one way to really understand a plant is to be involved in its propagation. This way you can observe its growth patterns, and any associated problems, through every stage of development. Invariably, the best-looking plants in my garden were introduced as small plants. The personal attention and nurturing I gave them has been paid off with a garden full of elegant, healthy plants. There are two ways of reproducing plants; by vegetative propagation or from seed.

## VEGETATIVE PROPAGATION

By this method you remove part of the parent plant, pot it up, and grow it on. The resulting plant will have identical characteristics to the parent plant.

### Palms

Palms are generally propagated by seeds; some species are capable of division, but not before adequate roots have developed. You can cut off the canes of *Rhapis multifida* and *Chamaedorea microspadix* at their roots and repot them. Treat any cut areas with fungicide. Occasionally these plants are reproduced through air layering. To do this thinly, slice 2cm (¾in) off the stem of the plant about 30cm (12in) from the end of the stem. Wrap damp moss around this area to cover the cut completely. Wrap a layer of polythene around this moss and keep it in place with elastic bands. Within a few months, and given adequate temperatures – at least 15°C (59°F) – roots should begin to develop. When sufficient roots have formed, cut the stem just below the point from which they are growing, and pot in a free-draining compost. In time, the roots will fill the pot and you will have a new plant.

## Yuccas

Most species create offsets on their rhizomes or stems. Leave offsets to develop adequate roots before removing them from the parent plant and dipping in hormone rooting powder. Stem cuttings can be taken during periods of active growth. Grow these in moist but not excessively wet sand and they will root up within a few months. Treat any cut areas with fungicide.

## Agaves

Many common *Agave* species form offsets from their rhizomes readily and, more infrequently, from the top part of their stem. The time at which these offsets form varies between the species, ranging from when the plant is still juvenile to the age at which it first flowers; this may vary by decades. Once an offset has developed sufficient roots, you can often simply pull it from the parent plant, though sometimes you may need to cut it off, using secateurs or a sharp knife.

Agaves can also be propagated by bulbils. These grow on a bud at the bottom of the flowers and, in time, form roots. When a bulbil has at least two pairs of leaves, it can be cut from the parent plant and potted up in a sandy compost. Treat any cut areas of the bulbil and the parent plant with fungicide.

## Cordylines

Non-green varieties are especially intolerant of root movement, so if you take basal offsets in the spring, be careful not to disturb the roots of the mother plant unnecessarily. In addition, make sure the offset has sufficient roots to take in enough water and nutrients to support itself. Use a sharp knife to cut the offset from the parent plant. The cut area of the parent plant and the root area of the offset can be treated with fungicide. This is good practice that will minimize the chance of fungi growing, and at minimal cost.

PROPAGATION

## Phormiums and astelias

The youngest, outer parts of a plant usually grow away the best. If you leave propagated plants outside, it is worth cutting the top half of the leaves off large specimens: this will help to reduce wind rock which can inhibit rooting, and create spaces around the roots in which water can puddle and freeze in cold weather. Sandy compost will help the plants get through the first winter with the least problems as it will help them root up fast. Wind rock is less of a problem for plants growing in a protected environment such as a greenhouse.

The division of phormiums, such as this one in need of splitting, is relatively easy

When you divide the plant, make sure that each part has plenty of roots

# FROM SEED

Plants grown from seed will have very similar, but not identical characteristics to the parent plant. Seeds collected from a garden may not be pure as fertilization by a different species may occur.

## Palms

The key to successful seed germination is to use fresh seeds. If you pick the ripe seed from a tree you will need to scrape off the exterior fruit. Soaking the fruit, for up to a week, will soften it and make this job easier. Change the soaking water daily to stop fermentation. You can even put some fungicide in the water. Always follow the manufacturers' instructions: too much of anything will eventually cause toxicity.

If you buy seed dry in a packet, soak it in the same way. This will help to remove the naturally occurring toxins that suppress germination. If you think the seeds have been attacked by boring beetles, soak them in an insecticide for half an hour, rinse them off well, then soak them in a fungicide to prevent damping off (fungus forming on the surface of the compost).

Use fast-draining compost in which to grow the seed. Sprinkle the surface with sand to reduce the chance of moss growing, as this will compete with the seedling for water and nutrients. The rate at which seeds germinate varies greatly from palm to palm – some take weeks, others years – so don't throw seeds away unless you are sure they are not going to germinate. A popular method of encouraging seeds to germinate is to put them in a plastic bag filled with damp, well-drained compost that has been soaked in a water-soluble fungicide such as Thiram. Seed originating from areas with a temperate or cool climate can be germinated at a temperature between 24 and 27°C (75 and 81°F). Palms from warmer areas require a temperature between 27 and 32°C (81 and 90°F).

When large enough to handle, seedlings can be transplanted to 10cm (4in) pots. At this stage, fortnightly liquid feeds will accelerate growth. Add a slow-release fertilizer to the compost mix when you repot.

## Cycads

Propagation is from seeds. Sow seeds in spring at a temperature between 15° and 29°C (60° and 85°F), in a free-draining compost.

## Yuccas and agaves

The seeds of yuccas and agaves usually germinate quickly, often within a few weeks of sowing. They tend to store well when kept dry and remain viable for many years. You are more likely to get pure seeds if you buy them: if there are a number of

This is a good size for palm seedlings to be potted up

yuccas in or near your garden, the seeds may have been pollinated by other species. To be sure you get the plant you want, you can hand-pollinate a yucca by brushing pollen onto the stigma.

Seeds should be grown in a very fast-draining compost of perlite and vermiculite to remain moist. As the particles of perlite and vermiculite are large, water will drain through them freely. However, they have the capacity to hold water which can be drawn out by dry organic matter that plant roots can then tap. This is generally enough to keep the roots moist, but not sodden. Any more moisture than this may rot the seeds. Germination will be quicker if the seeds are kept in bright, indirect light and temperatures remain above 27°C (81°F).

The rate at which plants mature depends upon the individual species. While agaves and yuccas don't need much fertilizer as mature plants, adding fertilizer from an early age will help them bulk up. As the plants mature, gradually expose them to higher light levels.

## Cordylines

Cordylines don't need such a free-draining compost as agaves and yuccas, but it may still be worth adding sand to a standard compost as this aids rooting. As with agaves and yuccas, you are more likely to get pure seeds if you buy them, as cordylines can also hybridize easily. Mind you, the resulting plants may have interesting and unique features and I have grown some green hybrids that romped away. However, this easy cross-pollination can cause problems when specimens of different colours are grown next to each other as their sizes can vary so much, giving an unbalanced look to a garden. Seeds germinate around 15°C (60°F) and are best sown in the spring.

## Phormiums

Once again, easy hybridization produces highly variable plant sizes and colours. This is particularly noticeable with purple types. Plants grown from the same seed mix can range in size from 50cm to 2m (1ft 4in to 6ft 6in). Still, this allows you to grow a plant just the right height for its eventual location. Seeds germinate readily in seed compost within a few months. Spring is the best sowing time, in temperatures around 20°C (68°F).

# CHAPTER SIX

# BUYING SPECIMEN PLANTS

Not only do one or two specimen plants give a garden a mature look, they also act as a focal point. Unfortunately, cost usually prohibits us from buying as many as we would like. I have been collecting palms and palm-like plants since the 1980s and, as a garden contractor, I buy hundreds of plants each year. Through this hands-on experience I have learnt much – I hope the following observations will help you decide which plants are worth buying, and why.

The dramatic shape of these agaves is eye-catching

# CONTAINER-GROWN OR CONTAINERIZED

If specimens are not properly rooted and watered after being containerized (potted up after having been grown in the ground) they may dry out, and any subsequent long journeys can cause much stress to the plants. The result may be that a large section of the roots dies, even though the leaves will look reasonable for some time. If possible, always check the roots before buying a containerized plant.

Large specimens that were growing 'in the wild' before being containerized need to develop healthy roots in the pot before being planted in garden soil. If you are unsure whether a specimen is ready for planting out, cut a hole in the pot and look to see if the roots are adequately formed; if you can turn the pot upside down and remove the plant with no compost falling away, it is ready. If it isn't ready, you can always sink the pot in the ground until the plant has rooted thoroughly. Such plants often take several years to get going and to match the appearance of plants that have been nurtured from germination. For this reason, container-grown plants tend to be better value than containerized ones, but they can be difficult to locate; as there may be no large container-grown plants available, and remembering how long it takes to grow sizeable plants, an imperfect containerized one may be an acceptable compromise.

## Special deals

The price of a plant can compensate for any imperfections it may have. I bought a couple of 1.5m (5ft) *Phoenix canariensis* palms, with trunks 30cm (1ft) wide and 35cm (1ft 1½in) high, very cheaply because their leaves were far from perfect, but they had the potential to become sizeable plants within a few years. It is always worth keeping an eye out for such special deals. Winter is often a good time to buy expensive plants that you've had your eye on as many businesses have sales with up to 25 per cent off their normal prices.

# PLANTING OUT

Palm-like plants are frequently grown in warm rather than temperate climates to maximize their rate of growth. If they are grown in a warmer climate, or in the greenhouses of temperate nurseries, make sure they have been hardened off properly before you plant them outside.

Although palms can grow in containers for many years without serious problems, like all plants, their roots need freedom for the plant to grow at its best. Check the roots of any plants you buy and if they are pot-bound, try to tease them out. The bigger the plant, the tougher the roots. Perseverance will pay off in the long run, with quicker-growing plants. *Trachycarpus fortunei*, *Chamaerops humilis* and *Phoenix canariensis* are usually available as sizeable palms, at reasonable prices, and as they are such fast sellers there is less chance of their being pot-bound.

When digging a hole for a new plant, try to dig as deep as the roots and then at least half as deep again, and allow a similar distance around the sides. Break up the bottom of the hole with a fork to aid root penetration. When planting from a pot, the base of the trunk should be level with the garden soil.

To avoid damaging the leaves of a new palm, take care to acclimatize it to sunlight. Unless you know it has been growing in a sunny position, you should expose the plant to more sunlight gradually by moving it into an increasingly sunny position over a period of months. If the leaves blacken or turn yellow, you are moving it too quickly. The smaller the plant, the more time it will take. Some palms don't like sunlight at all and within a few days of exposure, their leaves will be badly damaged. *Chamaedorea radicalis* is badly affected but yuccas, cordylines and phormiums suffer less.

The yellowing and black ends on the leaves of this *Chamaedorea radicalis* are due to the plant being moved too rapidly into a position with more sunlight

# WHAT TO LOOK FOR

Where possible, look for plants with no weed growth in the surface compost. When the leaves of green plants are pale, this usually indicates a deficiency of nitrogen and may also indicate general poor care.

If you are looking to grow the most beautiful plants, small is beautiful should be your motto: the most attractive plants in my garden started off as small specimens.

Some rare plants can be hard to grow and may appear imperfect; remember that someone may have crossed half the planet to collect the seeds and don't be overly critical.

## Cycads

Small specimens of *Cycas revoluta* are not too expensive but other cycads, and even *C. revoluta* with only a 30cm (1ft) trunk, are not cheap.

## Yuccas and agaves

Most yuccas and agaves are slow-growing but the larger they get, the greater the chance of their becoming pot-bound. While they tend to live healthily in pots due to their low nutritional and water needs, they normally don't reach their full size unless they are planted in the ground.

This group planting of *Cycas revoluta* specimens of differing heights creates a pleasing outline

## Cordylines

Cordylines form wood fairly slowly so large plants can easily become pot-bound. However, with cordylines I generally avoid teasing the roots out much as for them it seems to do more harm than good – and even plants without a trunk can look spectacular.

## Phormiums and astelias

When buying phormiums and astelias, avoid tall (1m; 3ft 3in) specimens with only a few leaves unless you want to fill a specific hole in a border and the price is no more than that of a smaller, clumping plant. The problem is that these large, single-leaved specimens rarely bulk-up quickly. Either buy a small, bushy plant or pay more for a bushy specimen plant.

SECTION TWO

# DISPLAY

HARD LANDSCAPING

COMPANION PLANTING AND GARDEN STYLES

# CHAPTER SEVEN

# HARD LANDSCAPING

Using paints, tiles and pavers in your garden will help you realize the full potential of your plants. Even a few well-chosen pots can radically alter the mood.

## PAINTS

Setting appealing colours and landscaping around your plants will help to bring out their full potential. You can use colourful paint to suggest a warmer climate; Moroccan blue has often been used to create an Arabian atmosphere. Pastel shades are often utilized in tropical countries. In fact, soft blues, pinks and greens are favoured in countries as diverse as Peru and India. A particularly good use of pastels can be found in the Art Deco area of Miami where walls are painted in Art Deco designs using these soft colours.

## TILES

Terracotta floor tiles are especially effective in Mediterranean-style gardens, and glazed tiles decorated with motifs could be used on step risers. Depending upon the design, a Spanish or even Arab flavour can be achieved with these. Tiles can also be used to adorn planters. However you use them, consideration must be given to their frost-hardiness. Ceramic tiles are frost-hardy but offer the least choice of designs. Single-fired

In Mediterranean countries, most notably in Spain and Portugal, painted tiles are often used to decorate park benches, steps and planters

terracotta tiles are less frost-hardy but offer a greater choice of design. Double-fired terracotta tiles are the least frost-hardy. If you use these, you will need to apply a clear sealant to the unglazed parts to give them some protection. This will help to stop them shattering when exposed to freezing temperatures.

# FENCES AND PAVING

Fences, and indeed any woodwork, can be painted to help set the character of your garden. Bamboo screens will add an oriental flavour. The type of paving you lay will also contribute to the mood. It can be riven or even flecked, which can resemble marble. You can add contrast by using edging stones in a different colour.

A herringbone pattern adds interest to the paved area of this garden

43

# LIGHTING

Increasingly, gardens are used as outside rooms in which to entertain and relax. To capitalize on the sculptural qualities of your plants, use a range of garden lighting. By exploring different angles you will find the optimal position to create the best effect. However, if you over-illuminate, you may lose some of the architectural definition of your plants.

Lighting can be directed in one of three main ways:

* uplighting: from the middle of the plant or just in front of it, up and into it, to emphasize the underside of the plant
* downlighting: from above the plant, to light up the branches and emphasize the top of the plant
* spotlighting: focused on a particular point, to emphasize a specific plant

The range of pots available gives you the freedom to select a very particular style and design. This is a *Trachycarpus wagnerianus*.

# POTS

Terracotta pots come in a wide range of designs and sizes, but if your pots are to be used in a position where they might catch the wind, use wood or reconstituted stone planters instead as they are less likely to be knocked over. They can be painted to suggest a specific exotic style. Some glazed pots are decorated with motifs that would suit an oriental style.

I like to enjoy my palms right from their day of purchase. Small specimens can be left in their pots and countersunk into containers so that their roots don't have to compete with those of surrounding plants. If you plant out in summer, do make sure that your plants have acclimatized to the sun though, or their leaves

may burn. The hotter it is when you plant them out, the greater the need for careful acclimatization. If you plant out in winter, you will need to acclimatize them to the cold.

Whether as specimen plants or in mixed plantings, palms and spiky plants will help create a specific mood on any patio. They can be placed in corners, as sentinels at the entrance of stairs and doors, or in the centre of island plantings. One of the best palms for use in containers is *Chamaerops humilis*. Its clumping nature quickly produces a very bushy appearance. The blue cultivar *C. h.* 'Cerifera' is particularly striking. *Washingtonia filifera* is an affordable choice and looks good both in a container and as a dot plant in bedding schemes. It is known as the cotton palm because of the filaments at the tips of its leaves.

Small specimens of *Phoenix canariensis* and *Trachycarpus fortunei* can be used to centre up pots (planted in the centre with the object of surrounding it with other plants): if they become too big they can be transplanted into the garden. Always take care to place large specimens, such as *Trachycarpus fortunei*, in pots that are big enough to withstand the force of wind on them and keep from blowing over: *T. fortunei* isn't called the windmill palm for nothing. *Trachycarpus wagnerianus* is often better for pot culture as its compact nature is beautifully proportioned, and less susceptible to the ravages of wind.

The siting and shape of the pot can also contribute to its 'wind-resistance' – square pots are less likely to blow over in a corner.

Plants with a vertical habit, such as phormiums and cordylines, will soon enhance a boring niche. Underplanted cordylines in urns will provide a decorative entrance to steps. Even hanging baskets can be centred-up with juvenile plants, though if they are used in an exposed site, they may need protection in harsh weather. They can be moved temporarily to a less exposed site, wrapped in fleece or packed with straw.

A point will come when it is no longer practical to pot a plant on, and it will have to be put into open ground. Any plant larger than 1m (3ft 3in) tall will invariably grow faster in the ground than in a pot.

# CHAPTER EIGHT

# COMPANION PLANTING AND GARDEN STYLES

Why do people grow palms and spiky plants in their gardens? Usually they are looking for a bold leaf shape that will contrast well with other plants or whose architectural shape makes it a fine specimen plant. Working the other way round, tropical plants are often the first choice to use alongside palms and spiky plants and they complement them very effectively.

As palms are relatively slow-growing, you can vary the plants you grow with them as they get larger; herbaceous plants and low-growing shrubs may be the most appropriate initially, but as the palms grow, larger plants may look more in proportion.

In this mixed bed, palms and phormiums are planted with colourful annuals

Conifers, especially open-branched species such as *Pinus sylvestris*, work well with palms and can give a Mediterranean feel to any planting. Their foliage offers a wide selection of greens and there are also superb blue, yellow and variegated forms. Some even turn russet over winter. As the ultimate height of different species varies greatly, there will always be one to match the height of a plant you have.

The planting along this driveway at a palm centre combines palms and other spiky plants with the vertical form of conifers

A multitude of annuals and ground covers can be planted around palms, whether they are in a planter or in open ground. If you use annuals you can vary the leaf shapes and colours to give your garden a fresh look each year.

While familiar plants such as impatiens work well alongside the plants listed in the Directory, there are dozens of unusual alternatives. I have grown a short variety of variegated nasturtium – 'Alaska', 25cm (10in) in height – in front of a bed of palms and spiky plants to great effect. A *Cerinthe major* 'Purpurascens' growing in the same bed contrasted well against my red and variegated phormiums.

By looking through a good seed catalogue you will find a massive range of plants with which to make your beds highly individual. Indeed, you will search for a long time before finding a group of plants that offer such scope for companion planting, whether with annuals, herbaceous plants, shrubs or trees. Your imagination can run riot as you stamp your personality onto your garden with your own particular choice.

# EXOTIC TEMPERATE GARDEN

Whatever style of garden you have, the architectural shape of palms and spiky plants will help you create drama. They can captivate the imagination and definitely lend themselves to adventurous planting. Below I have listed suitable plants for exotic temperate gardens in general, along with some ideas for more specific considerations, including shaded areas and jungle-style gardens.

By using primarily evergreen plants, you can make this type of garden interesting all year long. While non-hardy, large-leaved plants, such as bananas, can be included, their lack of leaves in winter shouldn't radically affect the overall appearance. In this garden style, different textures and brightly coloured foliage abounds and by planting a wide range of colourful shrubs, trees and herbaceous plants to complement the powerful architectural shapes of palms and spiky plants, you will have an exotic look year-round. Try a range of colour contrasts, for example, silver next to red and blue alongside yellow.

## Complementary trees

A magnolia with red on the underside of the leaf will provide good contrast in a vertically tiered bed when a variegated shrub is grown in front of it.

*Ficus carica* 'Brown Turkey' (green foliage)
*Catalpa bignonioides* 'Aurea' (yellow foliage)
*Cercis canadensis* 'Forest Pansy' (red foliage)
*Eucalyptus glaucescens* (blue foliage)
*Magnolia grandiflora* (green foliage)

Eucalyptus glaucescens

Magnolia grandiflora

*Olea europaea* (silver foliage)

*Acer palmatum* 'Atropurpureum' (red foliage)

*Acacia dealbata* (green foliage)

## Complementary conifers

Conifers work surprisingly well alongside the plants listed in the Directory. This is particularly true of the open-branching types of pinus: as their size and colour vary so greatly they can be 'matched' with different specimens.

*Chamaecyparis* 'Golden Mopp' (yellow foliage)

*Juniperus squamata* 'Blue Star' (blue foliage)

*Pinus sylvestris* 'Gold Coin' (yellow foliage)

*Picea kosteri* 'Glauca' (blue foliage)

*Araucaria araucana* (green foliage)

*Ginkgo biloba* (green foliage)

*Cypressus sempervirens* (green foliage)

*Pinus sylvestris*

*Picea kosteri*

# Complementary shrubs

As shrubs are the backbone of most gardens, making the correct choice is critical. By selecting those with interesting foliage, especially evergreen varieties, you can contrast colours and forms elegantly with your palms and spiky plants. Some, such as *Fatsia japonica* and *Hydrangea aspera*, have large, bold leaves while others, including *Prunus laurocerasus* 'Marbled White' and *Pittosporum tenuifolium* 'Irene Paterson', have subtle, marbled foliage.

### Red shrubs

*Photinia* x *fraseri* 'Red Robin'

*Pittosporum tenuifolium* 'Purpureum'

*Berberis thunbergii* f. *atropurea*

*Nandina domestica*

*Cotinus coggygria* 'Royal Purple'

*Weigela florida* 'Foliis Purpureis'

*Photinia* x *fraseri* 'Red Robin'

*Pittosporum tenuifolium* 'Purpureum'

### Yellow shrubs

*Choisya ternata* Sundance = 'Lich'

*Weigela* Rubidor (syn. *W.* Briant Rubidor = 'Olympiade')

*Pittosporum tenuifolium* 'Warnham Gold'

*Euonymus japonicus* 'Ovatus Aureus'

*Cornus alba* 'Aurea'

*Ligustrum ovalifolium* 'Aureum'

*Choisya ternata* Sundance = 'Lich'

*Euonymus japonicus* 'Ovatus Aureus'

### Variegated shrubs

*Griselina littoralis* 'Dixon's Cream'
*Pittosporum tenuifolium* 'Irene Paterson'
*Prunus laurocerasus* 'Marbled White'
*Aucuba japonica* 'Crotonifolia'
*Fuchsia venusta* 'Versicolor'
*Elaeagnus x ebbingei* 'Eleador'

*Griselina littoralis* 'Dixon's Cream'

*Prunus laurocerasus* 'Marbled White'

## Silver shrubs

*Cytisus battandieri*
*Teucrium fruticans*
*Convolvulus cneorum*
*Elaeagnus angustifolia*
*Senecio greyi* hort.
*Lavandula* spp.

*Teucrium fruticans*

*Convolvulus cneorum*

## Green shrubs

*Hydrangea aspera*
*Rhododendron sinogrande*
*Callistemon citrinus*
*Fatsia japonica*
*Mahonia x media* 'Charity'
*Choisya* 'Aztec Pearl'

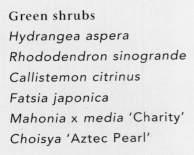

*Fatsia japonica* leaf

*Mahonia x media* 'Charity'

# Complementary herbaceous plants

There are many hardy herbaceous plants with exceptional foliage. The advantages in using them are that they don't need moving in winter and many keep their foliage during this time. Some plants, among them *Cynara cardunculus*, have beautiful cut leaves while others, such as *Ajuga reptans* 'Multicolor', form fascinating ground covers.

### Red herbaceous plants
*Sedum telephium* subsp. *maximum* 'Atropurpureum'
*Heuchera micrantha* var. *diversifolia* 'Palace Purple'
*Tellima grandiflora* 'Purpurea'
*Ajuga reptans* 'Catlin's Giant'
*Bergenia cordifolia* 'Purpurea'
*Tiarellia wherryi* 'Bronze Beauty'

### Yellow herbaceous plants
*Lamium maculatum* 'Aureum'
*Tradescantia* 'Chedglow'
*Stachys byzantina* 'Primrose Heron'
*Filipendula ulmaria* 'Aurea'
*Melissa officinalis* 'Aurea'
*Valeriana phu* 'Aurea'

*Heuchera micrantha* var. *diversifolia* 'Palace Purple'

*Ajuga reptans* 'Catlin's Giant'

*Lamium maculatum* 'Aureum'

*Tradescantia* 'Chedglow'

**Variegated herbaceous plants**
*Bergenia cordifolia* 'Tubby Andrews'
*Persicaria virginiana* 'Painter's Palette'
*Pulmonaria rubra* 'David Ward'
*Brunnera macrophylla* 'Variegata'
*Sedum alboroseum* 'Frosty Morn'
*Heuchera* 'Helen Dillon'
*Pachysandra terminalis*

Pachysandra terminalis

Bergenia cordifolia 'Tubby Andrews'

**Silver herbaceous plants**
*Cynara cardunculus*
*Artemisia ludoviciana*
*Lamium maculatum* 'White Nancy'
*Echinops ritro*
*Veronica spicata* subsp. *incana*
*Eryngium giganteum*

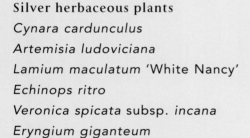

Cynara cardunculus

Artemisia ludoviciana

**Green herbaceous plants**

*Arisaema* spp.
*Lysichiton americanus*
*Veratrum nigrum*
*Euphorbia myrsinites*
*Acanthus mollis*
*Agapanthus* spp.

Veratrum nigrum

The glorious blue of an *Agapanthus*

**Hardy, large-leaved herbaceous plants**

*Gunnera manicata*
*Zantedeschia aethiopica* 'Crowborough'
*Hosta* 'Big Daddy'
*Rheum palmatum*
*Rodgersia tabularis*
*Farfugium* spp.

Gunnera manicata

Zantedeschia aethiopica 'Crowborough'

Non-hardy, large-leaved herbaceous plants

*Musa basjoo*

*Ensete ventricosum* 'Maurelii'

*Canna* 'Durban'

*Canna* 'Striata'

*Tetrapanax papyrifer*

*Ricinus* 'Gibsonii'

*Canna 'Durban'*

*Musa basjoo*

## Complementary ferns

As ferns grow to between 10cm and 4m (4in and 13ft) high, different species associate well with a wide range of the plants listed in the Directory. Generally, most prefer to be out of the midday sun. If you are looking for something several metres tall, grow the Australian tree fern *Dicksonia antarctica*. The silver-leaved *Athyrium niponicum* var. *pictum* has particularly striking leaves. The evergreen *Blechnum chilense* looks very exotic.

Evergreen ferns

*Asplenium scolopendrium*

*Blechnum chilense*

*Blechnum spicant*

*Polypodium vulgare*

*Cyrtomium falcatum*

*Polystichum aculeatum*

*Asplenium scolopendrium*

*Blechnum chilense*

**Deciduous ferns**
*Dicksonia antarctica*
*Polystichum setiferum*
*Athyrium niponicum*
*Osmunda regalis*
*Dryopteris filix-mas*
*Matteuccia struthiopteris*

*Polystichum setiferum*

*Dicksonia antarctica*

# Complementary grasses

Grasses can be used in an informal jungle-style garden and in more formal Mediterranean-style gardens. Their vertical form contrasts well with differently shaped plants. What makes them interesting and useful is the wide range of sizes and colours in which they are available. In addition, a number are evergreen and so provide year-round interest.

**Green grasses**
*Arundo donax*
*Miscanthus sinensis*

**Yellow grasses**
*Carex elata* 'Aurea'
*Deschampsia flexuosa* 'Tatra Gold'

**Variegated grasses**
*Carex oshimensis* 'Evergold'
*Phalaris arundinacea* var. *picta*
*Cortaderia selloana* 'Aureolineata'
*Arundo donax* var. *versicolor*

*Arundo donax*

*Carex oshimensis* 'Evergold'

*Cortaderia selloana 'Aureolineata'*

**Red grasses**
*Uncinia rubra*
*Imperata cylindrica 'Rubra'*
*Hakonechloa macra 'Aureola'*

**Blue grasses**
*Festuca glauca*
*Elymus magellanicus*
*Helictotrichon sempervirens*

**Black grasses**
*Ophiopogon planiscapus 'Nigrescens'*

*Ophiopogon planiscapus 'Nigrescens'*

*Uncinia rubra*

59

# Complementary bamboos

These graceful, vertical plants are available in a range of
heights, leaf sizes, and leaf and stem colours that gives you a
massive selection from which to choose, no matter what you
wish to combine them with.

**Large-leaved bamboos**
*Sasa palmata*
*Indocalamus tessellatus*

**Variegated-leaved bamboos**
*Pleioblastus shibuyanus* 'Tsuboi'
*Sasaella masamuneana* f. *albostriata*

*Sasaella masamuneana f. albostriata*

*Pleioblastus shibuyanus 'Tsuboi'*

**Coloured-stemmed bamboos**
*Phyllostachys aurea* (yellow)
*Phyllostachys nigra* (black)

*Phyllostachys nigra*

*Phyllostachys aurea*

## Complementary climbers

Climbers can be grown up house walls where they can display an interesting colour contrast with palms and spiky plants growing in front of them. Annual climbers can even be grown up palms without smothering them or competing with the tree's roots, especially if the climbers are grown in a surface mulch.

Evergreen climbers
*Clematis armandii*
*Trachelospermum jasminoides* 'Variegatum'
*Pyracantha* 'Sparkler'
*Hedera helix* 'Goldheart'
*Lonicera japonica* 'Aureoreticulata'

*Trachelospermum jasminoides* 'Variegatum'

*Clematis armandii*

*Hedera helix* 'Goldheart'

### Deciduous climbers
*Solanum jasminoides* 'Album Variegatum'
*Passiflora caerulea*
*Campsis radicans*
*Clematis* hybrids
*Actinidia kolomikta*
*Jasminum officinale* 'Argenteovariegatum'

### Annual climbers
*Ipomoea tricolor* 'Heavenly Blue'
*Nasturtium*, variegated examples

*Solanum jasminoides* 'Album Variegatum'

Variegated nasturtium

Ivy growing in profusion around the trunk of a palm

A less unkempt covering of ivy

# MEDITERRANEAN-STYLE GARDENS

Silver-leaved plants such as *Olea europaea* (the ubiquitous olive tree) and *Teucrium fruticans* are typical of Mediterranean gardens, and conifers are also very widely planted. All of the plants listed in the Directory would be at home in a Mediterranean-style garden. To these could be added pencil-like conifers such as *Cypressus sempervirens*, clipped box, and silver plants such as lavender. Bananas could also be used to complement palms in this style of garden. Many Mediterranean gardens have a geometric design but as the term covers such a large and diverse area, there are many variations to this theme. Generally, the plants in this type of garden are planted further apart than in most exotic temperate gardens so that they stand alone, without merging into one another.

A Mediterranean-style garden combining conifers and olives with spiky plants

**Silver plants**

*Senecio* spp.
*Teucrium fruticans*
*Cytisus battandieri*
*Cytisus* spp.
*Santolina* spp.
*Lavandula* spp.
*Astelia* spp.
*Olea europaea*
*Convolvulus cneorum*
*Phlomis* spp.

**Variegated plants**

*Myrtus* spp.
*Yucca* spp.
*Cordyline* spp.
*Phormium* spp.

Majestic palms among mixed planting
evoke hot Mediterranean climes

**Blue-leaved plants**

*Eucalyptus gunnii*
*Elymus magellanicus*
*Festuca glauca*

**Green-leaved plants**

*Cyperus sempervirens*
*Tamarix* spp.
*Hibiscus* spp.
*Citrus* spp.
*Buxus* spp.
*Taxus* spp.
*Ficus* spp.
*Hebe* spp.
*Callistemon* spp.

**Climbers**

*Jasminum* spp.
*Passiflora* spp.
*Vitis* spp.

# SHADED GARDENS

While most people tend to think of palms and spiky plants as sun-loving tropical plants, quite a number actually prefer shade. I have grown healthy specimens of *Astelia nervosa* and *Trachycarpus wagnerianus* with no direct sun for many years; it appears that the only result is that they grow more slowly. *Chamaedorea radicalis* and *C. microspadix* really only grow healthily in the shade. *Rhapis* palms, such as *R. multifida*, seem to grow best in the shade as well, and while most cordylines do not like excessive shade, *C. indivisa* grows naturally in open forest so it will tolerate modest shade. From my experience, the best yucca for shade is the green form of *Y. filamentosa*.

## Complementary shade-tolerant plants

Bamboos

Ferns

*Carex oshimensis* 'Evergold'

Fatsias

Hydrangeas

Mahonias

Pulmonarias

Lamiums

Ajugas

Heucheras

*Cordyline australis* and *Trachycarpus takil* growing happily in the shaded part of a garden

65

# JUNGLE-STYLE GARDENS

In addition to palms and spiky plants, large-leaved plants such as bananas, bamboos and ferns would be at the heart of such green garden settings. *Chamaedorea radicalis* would look at home on a jungle floor, which isn't surprising as it is a native of the Mexican highlands, but it does need to be grown in a shady site that is not exposed to heavy frosts.

A whole garden laid out in this style may hold limited appeal for most, but just one border can be planted up in this style. By concentrating on a mixture of green plants, including trees, shrubs and herbaceous plants, you can create the look of a rainforest or jungle. Close, tiered planting is at the heart of this style. Green-leaved climbers can ramble through shrubs and up trees, and large-leaved plants, such as gunneras and cannas, can abound, but as few of these are evergreen, a border filled with them may look bare in winter.

Bamboos
*Sasa palmata*
*Indocalamus* spp.
*Pseudosasa japonica*
*Fargesia nitida*

Large-leaved plants
*Canna* spp.
*Gunnera* spp.
*Zantedeschia aethiopica*
*Rheum* spp.

A lush growth, combining palms, spiky plants and broad leaves

**Grasses**
*Arundo donax*
*Cortaderia selloana*
*Miscanthus* spp.
*Carex* spp.

**Ferns**
*Dicksonia antarctica*
*Blechnum spicant*
*Asplenium scolopendrium*
*Dryopteris filix-mas*
*Polystichum setiferum*

Small, potted plants have been included to create this jungle style

SECTION THREE

# PLANT DIRECTORY

PALMS

◆

YUCCAS

◆

AGAVES

◆

CORDYLINES

◆

PHORMIUMS AND ASTELIAS

◆

MISCELLANEOUS SPIKY PLANTS

INDOOR PLANTS

# USING THE DIRECTORY

With the increasing popularity of sending plants through the post and the ever-expanding information available on the Web, the commercial availability of palms and spiky plants is improving every year. To give you a rough idea of the availability of particular species at this time, I have used the terms given below but, as with all things, as plant fashions change, so will availability.

◆ Very good – Usually available at garden centres
◆ Good – Sometimes available at garden centres, usually available at specialist nurseries
◆ Mediocre – Sometimes available at specialist nurseries
◆ Poor – Occasionally available at specialist nurseries
◆ Very poor – Usually only available in native environment

In each chapter I have included some of my personal favourites, but my main basis for selection was that the plants be commercially available, that they have good ornamental features, and that they are easy to grow. I have also included shade-tolerant species so that no corner of any garden need go unplanted. Combining a selection of these plants would create a kaleidoscope of leaf shapes and colours to challenge any collection found in warmer climates.

The clean shape of the agave instantly suggests the exotic

# CHAPTER NINE

# PALMS

Palms can be used effectively on patios, in mixed borders and as specimens in a lawn. While some require careful siting and maintenance, most will grow easily in the garden. If you are after a tropical look, they make perfect companions to bamboos, bananas and ferns. If you are searching for something that will make a strong statement in an otherwise bland border, palms can fill a variety of spaces. Even small Chusan palms will soon fill a 2m (6ft 6in) wide gap.

Few plants can be lit so effectively as their sculptural qualities create stunning shadows. And remember, as they are evergreen plants they will look great all year round. On a brooding winter's day, they will add colour and remind you that there is a summer to come.

Throughout recorded history, palms have played an important role in our lives. In the Middle East, the site of some of man's earliest towns, they were a source of both food and wood. As Jesus entered Jerusalem it was the humble palm leaf that carpeted the road and, to this day, palm leaves are shielded from the sun in order to provide blanched leaves for use in churches on Palm Sunday.

## PERSONAL FAVOURITES

### FEATHER

*Butia capitata*

*Phoenix canariensis*

*Jubaea chilensis*

*Phoenix theophrasti*

*Chamaedorea radicalis*

*Ceroxylon parvifrons*

### FAN

*Trachycarpus wagnerianus*

*Chamaerops humilis*

*Trachycarpus fortunei*

*Washingtonia filifera*

*Brahea armata*

*Rhapis excelsa*

The distinctive shape of palms can be combined with broadleaved and colourful plants to create a sense of profusion

## *Arenga engleri* – Formosa palm

An attractive feather palm named after the German botanist H. Engler

**Cold-hardiness**
To -4°C (25°F)

**Growth rate in temperate climates**
Slow

**Commercial availability**
Good

**Cultural requirements**
Well-drained, fertile soil; prefers partial shade

**Cold-weather protection**
Maximum; either grow in a pot and move to a more protected environment for winter or encase in straw during cold weather. Keep roots dry in winter

**Leaf**
Pinnate, green top with silvery underside

**Trunk**
Clumping, up to 4m (13ft) tall, but half this in a temperate climate

**Flower stalk**
Up to 70cm (6½in) long, with yellow flowers

**Fruit**
Red and toxic

**Propagation**
Germination erratic and slow, sometimes takes years

**Origin**
Taiwan

## *Arenga micrantha* – Bhutan fishtail palm

A new introduction that is the hardiest species of arenga

**Cold-hardiness**
To -6°C (21°F)

**Growth rate in temperate climates**
Slow to moderate

**Commercial availability**
Poor

**Cultural requirements**
Well-drained, fertile soil

**Cold-weather protection**
Maximum; either grow in a pot and move to a more protected site for winter or encase in straw during winter. Keep roots dry

**Leaf**
Pinnate, green top with whitish underside

**Trunk**
Single and fibrous. Three possible forms with trunks up to 8m (26ft)

**Flower stalk**
Up to 1m (3ft 3in), with yellow flowers

**Fruit**
Red and toxic

**Propagation**
Slow, erratic germination

**Origin**
Bhutan, Tibet and India

## *Brahea armata* – Blue hesper palm

One of the most attractive palms to grow in a temperate climate. Few hardy palms can match its sumptuous sky-blue leaves. Careful attention to siting is required as fast drainage and full sun are essential to produce the best trees

**Cold-hardiness**
To -10°C (14°F)

**Growth rate in temperate climates**
Slow

**Commercial availability**
Good

**Cultural requirements**
Excellent drainage and sun for most of the day; best grown in a pot if drainage is poor. Keep roots dry in winter

**Cold-weather protection**
Move pots close to house in harsh weather; provide increasing protection as temperatures drop below -3°C (27°F)

**Leaf**
Fan, bluish, up to 1m (3ft 3in)

**Trunk**
Single and fibrous, up to 12m (40ft) in native environment though much less in temperate regions

**Flower stalk**
Up to 2m (6ft 6in), with yellow flowers

**Fruit**
Brown

**Propagation**
Seed germination takes three to four months

**Origin**
Mexico

A mature tree in flower

# *Brahea edulis* – Guadalupe palm

Surprisingly hardy palm, useful for pot culture as it is slow growing

**Cold-hardiness**
To -10°C (14°F)

**Growth rate in temperate climates**
Slow

**Commercial availability**
Mediocre/good

**Cultural requirements**
Excellent drainage and sun for most of the day. Best grown in a pot when drainage is poor

**Cold-weather protection**
Keep roots dry in winter. Move pot specimens close to house in winter and provide extra cover in cold weather

**Leaf**
Fan, green

**Trunk**
Single and bare, up to 12m (40ft) in native environment though much less in temperate regions

**Flower stalk**
Up to 1.5m (4ft), with yellow flowers

**Fruit**
Black

**Propagation**
Seed germination takes three to six months

**Origin**
Guadalupe

## *Butia capitata* – Jelly palm

My favourite pinnate palm, it exemplifies the exotic. Excellent both in ground and tubs

**Cold-hardiness**
To -10°C (14°F)

**Growth rate in temperate climates**
Reasonably fast

**Commercial availability**
Generally good, though specific forms may only be available through seed

**Cultural requirements**
Any reasonably draining soil with sun for at least half the day

**Cold-weather protection**
Medium; provide increasing protection when temperatures drop below -4°C (25°F)

**Leaf**
Pinnate, green to glaucous, up to 1m (3ft 3in) and curving back on itself. The cultivar 'Strictor' is more erect

**Trunk**
Single and bare, up to 5m (16ft 6in).

**Flower stalk**
Up to 1m (3ft 3in), with yellow flowers

**Fruit**
Orange

**Propagation**
Seed germination slow, taking from four to six months

**Origin**
Southern Brazil

## *Butia* hybrids

These palms show a mixture of both parents' characteristics. Their seeds seem always to be sterile

*Butia capitata* x *Jubaea chilensis*
Create by cross-pollinating the above palms

*Butiagrus*

*Butia capitata* x *Syagrus romanzoffiana*

# *Butia eriospatha* – Woolly butia

Similar to *B. capitata* but the spathes are covered with brown wool-like fibre

**Cold-hardiness**
To -10°C (14°F)

**Growth rate in temperate climates**
Moderately fast

**Commercial availability**
Mediocre

**Cultural requirements**
Any reasonably draining soil with sun for at least half the day

**Cold-weather protection**
Medium; provide increasing protection when temperatures drop below -4°C (25°F)

**Leaf**
Pinnate, green to glaucous and curving back on itself

**Trunk**
Single and bare, up to 6m (19ft 6in) in native environment

**Flower stalk**
Up to 1m (3ft 3in), with yellow flowers

**Fruit**
Yellow

**Propagation**
Erratic; up to ten months for germination

**Origin**
Southern Brazil

The woolly spathe of *Butia eriospatha*

# *Butia yatay* – Yatay palm

An attractive, underused palm

**Cold-hardiness**
To -10°C (14°F)

**Growth rate in temperate climates**
Reasonably fast

**Commercial availability**
Mediocre/good

**Cultural requirements**
Any reasonably draining soil with sun for at least half the day

**Cold-weather protection**
Provide increasing protection when temperatures drop below -4°C (25°F)

**Leaf**
Pinnate, glaucous-green and curving back on itself

**Trunk**
Single and bare, up to 12m (40ft)

**Flower stalk**
Up to 1m (3ft 3in), with yellow flowers

**Fruit**
Yellow

**Propagation**
Erratic; germination can take up to ten months

**Origin**
Argentina, Paraguay, Uruguay

# *Caryota* 'Himalaya' – Himalayan fishtail

The leaf shape resembles a fishtail

**Cold-hardiness**
To -6°C (21°F)

**Growth rate in temperate climates**
Slow to medium

**Commercial availability**
Mediocre

**Cultural requirements**
Sunny, sheltered location in well-draining, humus-rich soil. Responds well to fertilizing

**Cold-weather protection**
Pot-grown specimens can be overwintered in a cold greenhouse; if grown in the ground, provide increasing protection as temperatures drop below -3°C (27°F)

**Leaf**
Fishtail, green

**Trunk**
Single and bare, up to 20m (65ft) in native environment, probably much less in temperate climate

**Flower stalk**
Up to 2m (6ft 6in), with yellow flowers

**Fruit**
Red to black

**Propagation**
Erratic; fresh seeds germinate within twelve months

**Origin**
Himalayas (northern India)

## *Ceroxylon alpinum* – Andean wax palm

An attractive but underused pinnate palm

**Cold-hardiness**
To -5°C (23°F)

**Growth rate in temperate climates**
Slow to medium

**Commercial availability**
Good

**Cultural requirements**
Fast-draining, moist, acidic soil.
Increase exposure to sun slowly

**Cold-weather protection**
Grow in a pot until 1–2m (3ft 3in–6ft
6in) tall. If planted outside, choose
the most sheltered position and
provide heavy protection against
frosts when temperatures drop below
-3°C (27°F)

**Leaf**
Pinnate, green

**Trunk**
Bare and coated with wax, up to 25m
(82ft) in native environment though
much smaller in temperate climate

**Flower stalk**
Up to 2m (6ft 6in), with yellow flowers

**Fruit**
Red/orange

**Propagation**
Fresh seeds germinate within five
months

**Origin**
Northern Andes

# *Ceroxylon ventricosum* – Andean wax palm

An attractive but underused pinnate palm

**Cold-hardiness**
To -6°C (21°F)

**Growth rate in temperate climates**
Medium

**Commercial availability**
Mediocre

**Cultural requirements**
Fast-draining, moist, acidic soil.
Increase exposure to sun slowly

**Cold-weather protection**
Grow in a pot until 1–2m (3ft 3in–6ft
6in) tall. If planted outside, choose the
most sheltered position and provide
heavy protection against frost when
temperatures drop below -3°C (27°F)

**Leaf**
Pinnate, green

**Trunk**
Bare and coated with wax, up to 30m
(98ft) plus in native environment
though much smaller in temperate
climate

**Flower stalk**
Up to 2m (6ft 6in), with yellow flowers

**Fruit**
Red

**Propagation**
Fresh seeds germinate within six
months

**Origin**
Northern Andes

## *Chamaedorea microspadix* – Bamboo palm

The stems have a bamboo-like appearance

**Cold-hardiness**
To -9°C (16°F)

**Growth rate in temperate climates**
Slow to medium

**Commercial availability**
Mediocre to good

**Cultural requirements**
Humus-rich soil with reasonable drainage. Grows best in total shade. Tolerates limited sunlight. Slugs love the foliage so I recommend protecting them against attack

**Cold-weather protection**
To grow the best leaves, wrap in fleece when temperatures drop below -3°C (27°F). Keep roots dry in winter

**Leaf**
Pinnate, green

**Trunk**
Clumping, up to 3m (10ft) in native environment though probably only 2m (6ft 6in) in temperate climate

**Flower stalk**
Up to 50cm (1ft 4in), with unremarkable yellow flowers

**Fruit**
Orange

**Propagation**
Fresh seeds germinate within four months

**Origin**
Mexico

# *Chamaedorea radicalis* – Hardy parlour palm

Delicate-looking understorey palm

**Cold-hardiness**
To -9°C (16°F)

**Growth rate in temperate climates**
Slow to medium

**Commercial availability**
Mediocre to good

**Cultural requirements**
Humus-rich soil with reasonable draining rate.
Grows best in shade. Considerable patience
required to acclimatize it to very limited sunlight

**Cold-weather protection**
To grow the best leaves possible, wrap in fleece
when temperatures drop below -3°C (27°F).
Keep roots dry in winter

**Leaf**
Pinnate, green

**Trunk**
Clumping, up to 4m (13ft) in native environment

**Flower stalk**
Up to 50cm (1ft 4in), with unexciting yellow
flowers

**Fruit**
Orange

**Propagation**
Fresh seeds take up to eight months to germinate

**Origin**
Mexico

# *Chamaerops Humilis* – Mediterranean or European Palm

Grows around the Mediterranean. Variable in growth habit: both single and multiple stemmed specimens are to be found, and occasionally variegated leafed cutlivars are encountered. The blue-leafed cultivar 'cerifera' comes from the Atlas Mountains of Morocco. A bushy cultivar comes from Mount Vesuvius in Italy and is marketed as 'volcano'. Sometimes the undersides of leaves are silvery green in colour.

**Cold-hardiness**
To -10°C (14°F)

**Growth rate in temperate climates**
Fairly fast to form a sizeable clumb, but slow to form trunks. Probably decades to form a 1m high trunk

**Commercial availability**
Good

**Cultural requirements**
Prefers sunny position, generally sun for at least half of the day. Dislikes poor drainage. Excellent for tub culture. Its bushy low-growing habit copes well with the wind

**Cold-weather protection**
Increasingly protect young palms and specimens that have not been hardened off when temperatures drop below -4°C (25°F)

**Leaf**
Fan, green 0.3–0.9m (1-3ft) in diameter. Leaf stalk has sharp spines

**Trunk**
Clumping

**Flower stalk**
Yellow flowers on short stalks coming from among the leaves

**Fruit**
Red, almost brown when ripe. Up to 2cm (¾ in) across

**Propagation**
Seeds usually need pollination from male and female specimens. Division possible when adequate roots are on an offset, but is slow to establish

**Origin**
Southern Europe and North Africa

## *Jubaea chilensis* – Chilean wine palm

An attractive palm, the leaves of which are a beautiful mid-green and of fine appearance. It is noted for its massive trunk. Kew Gardens in England holds the largest indoor example in the world

**Cold-hardiness**
To -10°C (14°F)

**Growth rate in temperate climates**
Slow, faster in the ground than in a pot

**Commercial availability**
Mediocre to good

**Cultural requirements**
Fast-draining soil in a sunny location

**Cold-weather protection**
Medium protection required when young, less as it matures

**Leaf**
Pinnate, green

**Trunk**
Bare, up to 25m (82ft)

**Flower stalk**
Up to 2m (6ft 6in), with yellow flowers

**Fruit**
Brown/yellow

**Propagation**
Erratic; germination can take over twelve months

**Origin**
Chile

## *Livistona australis* – Australian cabbage-leaf palm

Generally the best livistona to grow outside in a temperate climate

**Cold-hardiness**
To -5°C (23°F)

**Growth rate in temperate climates**
Slow to medium (this is the fastest-growing livistona)

**Commercial availability**
Mediocre to good

**Cultural requirements**
Sunny, very sheltered site in fast-draining soil

**Cold-weather protection**
Best grown in a pot that can be moved close to a house or in a cold greenhouse. Maximum protection against frost is essential

**Leaf**
Fan, green

**Trunk**
Bare, up to 30m (98ft) in native environment though much less in a temperate climate

**Flower stalk**
Up to 2m (6ft 6in), with yellow flowers

**Fruit**
Black/red

**Propagation**
Fresh seeds germinate within four months

**Origin**
Australia

*Livistona australis* has a very broad, fan-shaped leaf

# *Livistona chinensis* – Chinese fan palm

Best used as an indoor plant but it could be used outside in a pot during non-frosty periods

**Cold-hardiness**
To -3°C (27°F)

**Growth rate in temperate climates**
Slow to medium

**Commercial availability**
Mediocre to good

**Cultural requirements**
Grow in a well-drained pot and keep moist during warm periods

**Cold-weather protection**
Best grown in a pot that can be overwintered in a largely frost-free environment

**Leaf**
Fan, green

**Trunk**
Bare, up to 4m (13ft)

**Flower stalk**
Up to 1.5m (4ft), with yellow flowers

**Fruit**
Green/blue

**Propagation**
Fresh seeds germinate within three months

**Origin**
Japan and China

# Nannorrhops ritchiana – Mazari palm

The blue-leaved form is especially eye-catching

**Cold-hardiness**
To -10°C (14°F)

**Growth rate in temperate climates**
Slow

**Commercial availability**
Green form, poor; blue form, mediocre

**Cultural requirements**
Fast-draining soil in full sun if possible

**Cold-weather protection**
Best grown in a pot until large enough to put outside (10 years or more), then provide increasing protection as temperatures drop below -4°C (25°F). Keep roots dry in winter if possible

**Leaf**
Fan, green or blue

**Trunk**
Primarily subterranean, sometimes reaches 1–2m (3ft 3in–6ft 6in)

**Flower stalk**
Up to 1m (3ft 3in), with yellow flowers

**Fruit**
Red-brown

**Propagation**
Fresh seeds germinate within four months

**Origin**
Arabia to Pakistan

# *Parajubaea cocoides* – Coco cumbe

An attractive palm worth growing if the rare seeds of the hardier *P. torallyi* are unavailable

**Cold-hardiness**
To -4°C (25°F)

**Growth rate in temperate climates**
Moderate

**Commercial availability**
Plants, very poor; seeds, poor

**Cultural requirements**
Fast-draining soil in full sun. Unsuitable for pot culture as it creates a long tap root and if this is cut, it will kill the plant. If grown outside, a very sheltered site is essential. Dislikes excessively hot summers

**Cold-weather protection**
Maximum. By siting it between the corner of a house and a fence, a mini-greenhouse could be erected around it during the winter

**Leaf**
Pinnate, green top with silvery underside

**Trunk**
Single and bare

**Flower stalk**
Up to 1.5m (4ft), with yellow flowers

**Fruit**
Green/brown

**Propagation**
Slow and erratic, germination can take up to two years. To accommodate the tap root, I suggest using a 15 x 45cm (6 x 18in) pot for early years. Leave seed in a warm, dry place for several months before sowing

**Origin**
Ecuador and Colombia

## *Parajubaea torallyi* – Palma chico

An attractive, pinnate palm with considerable potential if well sited. In the wild, it grows at altitudes of up to 3,400m (1200ft), probably the highest altitude for palms in the world

**Cold-hardiness**
To -7°C (19°F)

**Growth rate in temperate climates**
Moderate

**Commercial availability**
Poor

**Cultural requirements**
Fast-draining soil in full sun. Unsuitable for pot culture as it creates a long tap root and if this is cut, it will kill the plant. If grown outside, a sheltered site is essential. Dislikes hot summers as it grows in an area where temperatures rarely rise above 23°C (73°F). Keep roots dry in winter and provide increasing protection when temperatures drop below -3°C (27°F)

**Cold-weather protection**
Maximum; encase in straw in harsh weather

**Leaf**
Pinnate, green top with grey-white underside

**Trunk**
Single and bare, to a height of 14 m (45ft)

**Flower stalk**
Up to 1.5m (4ft), with yellow flowers

**Fruit**
Green/grey

**Propagation**
Slow and erratic, up to two years.
To accommodate the tap root, I suggest using a 15 x 45cm (6 x 18in) pot for early years. Leave seed in a warm, dry place for several months before sowing

**Origin**
Bolivia

# *Phoenix canariensis* – Canary Island date palm

It will grow anywhere that has a climate ranging from dry tropical to temperate.
An inexpensive starter palm

**Cold-hardiness**
To -9°C (16°F)

**Growth rate in temperate climates**
Fast

**Commercial availability**
Very good; 'Timaru' (the hardiest cultivar), mediocre

**Cultural requirements**
Any well-drained soil with sun for at least half the day

**Cold-weather protection**
During the early years of growth, provide increasing protection when temperatures drop below -4°C (25°F)

**Leaf**
Pinnate, green

**Trunk**
Bare, up to 25m (82ft) in native environment

**Flower stalk**
Up to 2m (6ft 6in), with yellow flowers

**Fruit**
Yellow/orange

**Propagation**
Fresh seeds germinate within three months

**Origin**
Canary Islands

# *Phoenix theophrastii* – Cretan date palm

Distinctive foliage compared with *Phoenix canariensis*

**Cold-hardiness**
To -10°C (14°F)

**Growth rate in temperate climates**
Fast

**Commercial availability**
Mediocre to good

**Cultural requirements**
Any well-drained soil, with sun for at least half the day

**Cold-weather protection**
For the first few years after planting, provide increasing protection when temperatures drop below -4°C (25°F). It is essential to cover the growing apex in frosty weather; I use coarse bark, 10cm (4in) thick

**Leaf**
Pinnate, green

**Trunk**
Bare, up to 20m (65ft 6in) in native environment

**Flower stalk**
Up to 2m (6ft 6in), with yellow flowers

**Fruit**
Yellow/orange

**Propagation**
Fresh seeds germinate within four months

**Origin**
Crete and Turkey

# *Plectocomia himalayana* – Himalayan rattan palm

A climbing palm

**Cold-hardiness**
To -4°C (25°F)

**Growth rate in temperate climates**
Moderate

**Commercial availability**
Mediocre

**Cultural requirements**
A sheltered, fast-draining soil in a sunny position

**Cold-weather protection**
If climbing up a house, radiated heat should help substantially. Cover heavily with fleece in anything but the lightest frost

**Leaf**
Pinnate, green

**Trunk**
Thin, can grow to 10m (33ft) or more

**Flower stalk**
Beautiful, up to 2m (6ft 6in), with yellow flowers

**Fruit**
Yellow

**Propagation**
Fresh seeds should germinate within three months

**Origin**
Himalayas (northern India)

## *Rhapidophyllum hystrix* – Needle palm

One of the world's hardiest palms

**Cold-hardiness**
To -20°C (-4°F)

**Growth rate in temperate climates**
Very slow

**Commercial availability**
In USA, good; in Europe, mediocre

**Cultural requirements**
Preferably a sunny position but will tolerate some shade

**Cold-weather protection**
When young, protect in harsh weather

**Leaf**
Fan, green, up to 1m (3ft 3in) across

**Trunk**
Clumping and spiny

**Flower stalk**
Up to 1m (3ft 3in), with yellow flowers

**Fruit**
Brown

**Propagation**
Usually by division. Seed germination is erratic and can take up to eight months

**Origin**
South-east USA

# *Rhapis excelsa* – Lady palm

Wide variety of cultivars and variegated forms available for indoor use

**Cold-hardiness**
To -6°C (21°F)

**Growth rate in temperate climates**
Slow

**Commercial availability**
Green forms, good; variegated forms, poor

**Cultural requirements**
Well-draining soil in a largely shaded position or total shade

**Cold-weather protection**
Pot specimens can be moved to a cold greenhouse. If grown in the ground, provide increasing protection as temperatures drop below -3°C (27°F). Keep roots dry in winter

**Leaf**
Fan, green (variegated only if grown indoors)

**Trunk**
Clumping, thick canes up to 3m (10ft) in native environment

**Flower stalk**
Up to 60cm (24in), with yellow flowers

**Fruit**
White

**Propagation**
Fresh seed usually germinates within 10 weeks but is rarely available; for cultivars, propagation is by division

**Origin**
China

## *Rhapis humilis* – Slender lady palm

A good indoor and outdoor palm

**Cold-hardiness**
To -7°C (19°F)

**Growth rate in temperate climates**
Slow

**Commercial availability**
Mediocre

**Cultural requirements**
Well-drained soil in a largely shaded position

**Cold-weather protection**
Provide increasingly heavy protection when temperatures
drop below -3°C (27°F). Keep roots dry in winter

**Leaf**
Fan, green

**Trunk**
Clumping and thin, canes up to 5m (16ft 6in) in native environment

**Flower stalk**
Up to 70cm (28in), with yellow flowers

**Fruit**
None as all plants are male

**Propagation**
By division

**Origin**
China

## *Rhapis multifida* – Finger palm

A delicate looking shade loving palm.

**Cold-hardiness**
To -6°C (19°F)

**Growth rate in temperate climates**
Slow to moderate

**Commercial availability**
Mediocre

**Cultural requirements**
Good drainage preferably in indirect sunlight

**Cold-weather protection**
Cover with fleece when more than a degree or
two of frost is expected to keep the leaves in
good condition. Specimens next to a house seem
to do best

**Leaf**
Green. The cultivar 'china princess' is bushier in
appearance

**Trunk**
Clumping up to 2m (6ft 6in) high

**Flower stalk**
Short with yellow flowers

**Flower stalk**
Short with yellow flowers

**Propagation**
By seed or  division

**Origin**
China

# *Rhopalostylis sapida* – Nikau palm

Can only be grown in pots outside but its shade tolerance makes it an excellent house plant

**Cold-hardiness**
To -4°C (25°F), when mature

**Growth rate in temperate climates**
Slow

**Commercial availability**
Mediocre

**Cultural requirements**
Grow in a shaded position with well-draining compost. Acclimatize juvenile specimens to the sun slowly

**Cold-weather protection**
It is possibe that encasing mature plants (25 years plus) in straw could help keep them alive but move younger plants to the shelter of a greenhouse and keep temperatures above freezing. The cultivar 'Oceana', from the Chatham Islands, is the hardiest

**Leaf**
Pinnate, green. The top of this palm is shaped like a shaving brush and is very attractive

**Trunk**
Single and bare

**Flower stalk**
Up to 1.5m (4ft), with yellow flowers

**Fruit**
Red

**Propagation**
Fresh seed will germinate within four months

**Origin**
New Zealand

## *Sabal minor* – Dwarf palmetto

Largely trunkless north-American palm

**Cold-hardiness**
To -15°C (5°F)

**Growth rate in temperate climates**
Very slow

**Commercial availability**
Mediocre to good

**Cultural requirements**
Well-draining, humus-rich soil in full sun

**Cold-weather protection**
Unless it is a sizeable specimen, provide increasing protection when temperatures drop below -4°C (25°F). Keep roots dry in winter

**Leaf**
Fan, green to glaucous

**Trunk**
Mainly subterranean

**Flower stalk**
Up to 1m (3ft 3in), with fragrant yellow flowers

**Fruit**
Black

**Propagation**
Fresh seed germinates within four months

**Origin**
USA

# *Sabal palmetto* – Palmetto palm

A palm with a variable growing habit

**Cold-hardiness**
To -8°C (17°F)

**Growth rate in temperate climates**
Slow

**Commercial availability**
USA, good; Europe, mediocre

**Cultural requirements**
Well-draining soil in full sun.
Keep roots dry in winter

**Cold-weather protection**
Provide increasing protection when
temperatures drop below -3°C (27°F)

**Leaf**
Fan, green

**Trunk**
Single, up to 20m (65ft) in native
environment

**Flower stalk**
Up to 1.5m (4ft), with long yellow
flowers

**Fruit**
Black

**Propagation**
Fresh seed germinates within two
months

**Origin**
USA

# *Serenoa repens* – Saw palmetto

Dwarf palm with attractive non-green varieties

**Cold-hardiness**
To -7°C (19°F)

**Growth rate in temperate climates**
Slow

**Commercial availability**
Green forms, good; blue and silver forms, mediocre

**Cultural requirements**
Well-draining soil in sunny position. It is advisable not to move a larger specimen that has become established as this often leads to the death of the plant. If it is essential to move a plant, keep it well watered afterwards. Tolerates salty air

**Cold-weather protection**
Probably best grown in a pot until sizeable. Provide increasing protection for garden specimens when temperatures drop below -3°C (27°F). Keep roots dry in winter

**Leaf**
Fan, green, silver or blue according to variety

**Trunk**
Low, 1m (3ft 3in), bare and multi-trunked

**Flower stalk**
Up to 50cm (1ft 4in), with yellow flowers

**Fruit**
Black to dark blue

**Propagation**
For green and silver forms, fresh seed usually germinates within four months; blue varieties are usually propagated by division

**Origin**
USA

## *Syagrus romanzoffiana* – Queen palm

An attractive, pinnate palm

**Cold-hardiness**
To -4°C (25°F). *Syagrus macrocarpa* and *Syagrus botryophora* may prove to be more frost-hardy

**Growth rate in temperate climates**
Moderate

**Commercial availability**
Mediocre to good

**Cultural requirements**
Well-drained soil in full sun. A sheltered position is essential. Responds well to nitrogen

**Cold-weather protection**
Needs maximum protection, but a 2m (6ft 6in) specimen grows close to a house wall near where I live (in a zone 8 region) and has survived several winters. Keep roots dry in winter

**Leaf**
Pinnate, green

**Trunk**
Single and bare, up to 15m (49ft) in native environment

**Flower stalk**
Up to 2m (6ft 6in), with yellow flowers

**Fruit**
Orange

**Propagation**
Fresh seed germinates within four months

**Origin**
South America

## *Trachycarpus fortunei* – Chusan or windmill palm

Named after Robert Fortune, the nineteenth-century plant collector who first saw it on the Chinese island of Chusan. In England there are specimens over 100 years old

### Cold-hardiness
*Trachycarpus fortunei*, temperatures as low as -17°C (1.4°F); *T. f.* 'Hardy China', -20°C (-4°F); Bulgarian variety, -28°C (-18°F). This Bulgarian variety has no official name; it originated from seeds planted by Russians after WWII

### Growth rate in temperate climates
Fast; specimens with a 1m (3ft 3in) trunk can grow 30cm (1ft) per year

### Commercial availability
Very good

### Cultural requirements
Any soil with a reasonable rate of drainage. Tolerates shade up to two-thirds of the day. Responds well to regular fertilizing and watering

### Cold-weather protection
Provide increasing protection when temperatures drop below -6°C (21°F)

### Leaf
Fan, green, up to 1.2m (3ft 10in) across. The number of segments is variable, usually somewhere between 45 and 60

### Trunk
Single and fibrous, up to 15m (45ft).

### Flower stalk
Up to 1m (3ft 3in), with yellow flowers

### Fruit
Deep purple to black

### Propagation
Fresh seeds germinate within a few months; very rarely, a tree is a hermaphrodite, but it usually needs male and female trees for seed viability

### Origin
China

# *Trachycarpus latisectus* – Windermere palm

Named after the famous Windermere Sikkim Indian Hotel where a pair of these palms grows

**Cold-hardiness**
Uncertain, probably to -12°C (10°F)

**Growth rate in temperate climates**
Probably fast; specimens with a 1m (3ft 3in) trunk could grow up to 25cm (10in) per year

**Commercial availability**
Mediocre/Good and improving

**Cultural requirements**
Any adequately draining soil. Probably prefers more sun than *T. fortunei*. Should respond well to regular fertilizing and watering. Avoid exposure to excessive winds

**Cold-weather protection**
Medium; extra care must be taken until the trunk reaches 1m (3ft 3in)

**Leaf**
Fan, green, up to 1.2m (3ft 10in) across. Segments are more connected than those of *T. fortunei*

**Trunk**
Single and bare, up to 20m (65ft 6in)

**Flower stalk**
Up to 1m (3ft 3in), with yellow flowers

**Fruit**
Brown/black

**Propagation**
Fresh seeds germinate within a few months

**Origin**
Northern India

## *Trachycarpus martianus* – Khasia palm

One of the most attractive Trachycarpus species

**Cold-hardiness**
To -10°C (14°F), though this depends on the variety; the Nepalese form (no official name) is probably the hardiest, surviving temperatures at least a few degrees lower than the more common variety

**Growth rate in temperate climates**
Moderate

**Commercial availability**
Mediocre/good; certain forms are only available as seeds

**Cultural requirements**
Any reasonably draining soil

**Cold-weather protection**
Requires more protection than *T. fortunei*. Keep roots dry in winter and provide increasing protection when temperatures drop below -4°C (25°F)

**Leaf**
Fan, mid-green top with glaucous undersides, up to 1.2m (3ft 10in) across

**Trunk**
Single, usually bare but occasionally with fibres

**Flower stalk**
Up to 1m (3ft 3in), with yellow flowers

**Fruit**
Deep purple

**Propagation**
Fresh seeds germinate within three months

**Origin**
Nepal and north-eastern India

Juvenile *Trachycarpus martianus*

# *Trachycarpus oreophilus* – Thai mountain palm

This rare species is the least hardy form of Trachycarpus

**Cold-hardiness**
Probably to around -6°C (21°F)

**Growth rate in temperate climates**
Not very fast; specimens with a 1m (3ft 3in) trunk could grow 20cm (8in) per year

**Commercial availability**
Poor; seeds and seedlings are occasionally available

**Cultural requirements**
Faster-draining soil than other forms of Trachycarpus due to its natural, damp habitat – limestone ravine. Keep roots dry in winter. Avoid exposure to excessive winds

**Cold-weather protection**
Protect well when anything more than a light frost is expected, as it is a rare palm

**Leaf**
Fan, green top with a glaucous underside and up to 60 segments. The stalk is shorter than other trachycarpus species

**Trunk**
Single and bare, up to 12m (40ft)

**Flower stalk**
Up to 1m (3ft 3in), with yellow flowers

**Fruit**
Deep purple

**Propagation**
Fresh seeds germinate within four months

**Origin**
Northern Thailand

# *Trachycarpus princeps* – Stone Gate palm

The most recently discovered Trachycarpus, this has tremendous potential due to its attractive leaves

**Cold-hardiness**
Probably at least -14°C (7°F)

**Growth rate in temperate climates**
Reasonably fast

**Commercial availability**
Poor/very poor; seeds very occasionally available

**Cultural requirements**
Any reasonably draining soil

**Cold-weather protection**
Low but worth employing excessive measures to ensure success because of its rarity

**Leaf**
Fan, green top with white underside, up to 1m (3ft 3in) across. Between 30–50 per cent fewer segments than *T. fortunei*

**Trunk**
Single and fibrous, up to 8m (26ft), sometimes becomes bare with age

**Flower stalk**
Up to 1m (3ft 3in), with yellow flowers

**Fruit**
Deep purple

**Propagation**
Fresh seeds generally germinate within four months

**Origin**
Yunnan Province, China

# *Trachycarpus takil* – Kumaon palm

Similar in appearance to *T. fortunei*, the leaves can be a little larger. *Trachycarpus takil* can be identified by its twisted hatulas (the point where the leaf stalk breaks into segments)

**Cold-hardiness**
To -19°C (-2°F); reputedly slightly more hardy than *T. fortunei*

**Growth rate in temperate climates**
Fast; specimens with a 1m (3ft 3in) trunk could grow 30cm (1ft) per year

**Commercial availability**
Mediocre/good

**Cultural requirements**
Any adequately draining soil. Probably tolerates more shade than *T. fortunei* as its natural habitat is the shady side of a mountain

**Cold-weather protection**
Low, but provide increasing protection when temperatures drop below -6°C (21°F)

**Leaf**
Fan, dark green, up to 1.3m (4ft 3in) across

**Trunk**
Single up to 15m (45ft)

**Flower stalk**
Up to 1m (3ft 3in), with yellow flowers

**Fruit**
Deep purple to black

**Propagation**
Fresh seeds germinate within a few months; very rarely, a tree is a hermaphrodite, but it usually needs male and female trees for seed viability

**Origin**
Mount Thalkedar, northern India

# *Trachycarpus wagnerianus* – Short-leaved Chusan palm

Probably a sport (natural mutation) of Chinese origin, there are specimens over 100 years old in Japan. It is excellent for pot culture

**Cold-hardiness**
To -18°C (0°F)

**Growth rate in temperate climates**
Fast; specimens with a 1m (3ft 3in) trunk can grow 25cm (10in) per annum

**Commercial availability**
Good and improving. It has been crossed with *T. fortunei* and the resulting trees have variable leaf sizes

**Cultural requirements**
Any reasonably draining soil, it tolerates more shade than *T. fortunei*. Responds well to regular fertilizing and watering

**Cold-weather protection**
Provide increasing protection when temperatures drop below -6°C (21°F)

**Leaf**
Fan, green, up to 60cm (2ft) across and stiff

**Trunk**
Single with fibres, up to 8m (26ft) high

**Flower stalk**
Up to 1m (3ft 3in), with yellow flowers

**Fruit**
Deep purple to black

**Propagation**
Fresh seeds germinate within a few months; very rarely, a tree is a hermaphrodite, but it usually needs male and female trees for seed viability

**Origin**
China is thought to be most likely

## *Trithrinax acanthocoma* – Brazilian needle palm

Juvenile plants (up to eight years old) look like *T. fortunei* plants of the same age

**Cold-hardiness**
To -7°C (19°F)

**Growth rate in temperate climates**
Slow

**Commercial availability**
Mediocre

**Cultural requirements**
Well-draining soil in a sunny position. Keep roots dry in winter

**Cold-weather protection**
Provide increasing protection when temperatures drop below -3°C (27°F)

**Leaf**
Fan, green

**Trunk**
Fibrous and spiny, up to 3m (10ft)

**Flower stalk**
Up to 1.3m (4ft 3in), with white flowers

**Fruit**
White

**Propagation**
Fresh seed germinates within four months

**Origin**
Southern Brazil and Argentina

## *Trithrinax campestris* – Carandy palm

Mature leaves are incredibly hard and sharp

**Cold-hardiness**
To -10°C (14°F) for mature specimens

**Growth rate in temperate climates**
Slow

**Commercial availability**
Mediocre

**Cultural requirements**
Sunny position in well-draining soil. Keep roots dry
in winter

**Cold-weather protection**
Large specimens will not need much unless
temperatures drop below -6°C (21°F)

**Leaf**
Fan, grey to glaucous

**Trunk**
Usually clumping and spiny, up to 3m (10ft)

**Flower stalk**
Up to 1.3m (4ft 3in), with creamy-yellow flowers

**Fruit**
White

**Propagation**
Fresh seed germinates within four months

**Origin**
Northern Argentina and Uruguay

# *Washingtonia filifera* – American cotton palm

The usually relatively cheap price of this palm allows small specimens to be used in bedding schemes

**Cold-hardiness**
To -8°C (17°F)

**Growth rate in temperate climates**
Medium, fast with hot summers

**Commercial availability**
Good

**Cultural requirements**
Free-draining soil and sun for at least half the day

**Cold-weather protection**
Specimens with a trunk circumference of 90cm (3ft) and larger are worth protecting when temperatures drop below -5°C (23°F). Cover the growing apex with straw first and if temperatures continue to fall, cover the trunk. Smaller specimens should be encased in straw. Keep roots dry in winter

**Leaf**
Fan, green

**Trunk**
Single and bare, up to 15m (49ft) in their native environment

**Flower stalk**
Up to 5m (16ft 6in), with yellow flowers

**Fruit**
Black/brown

**Propagation**
Fresh seeds germinate within two months

**Origin**
Southern USA

113

# *Washingtonia robusta* – Mexican fan palm

The usually relatively cheap price of this palm allows small specimens to be used in bedding schemes

**Cold-hardiness**
Large specimen, to -6°C (21°F); small specimen, to -3°C (27°F)

**Growth rate in temperate climates**
Medium, fast in hot summers

**Commercial availability**
Good

**Cultural requirements**
Free-draining soil, in sun for at least half the day

**Cold-weather protection**
Specimens with a circumference of 90cm (3ft) and a larger trunk are worth protecting when temperatures drop below -4°C (25°F). Cover the growing apex with straw first and if temperatures continue to fall, cover the trunk. Smaller specimens should be encased in straw. Keep roots dry in winter

**Leaf**
Fan, green

**Trunk**
Single, up to 25m (82ft) in native environment

**Flower stalk**
Up to 3m (10ft), with yellow flowers

**Fruit**
Black/brown

**Propagation**
Fresh seeds germinate within two months

**Origin**
USA

Hair-like strands on a *Washingtonia robusta* leaf

*Washingtonia robusta*

115

# CHAPTER TEN

# YUCCAS

Many of these North American plants have been cultivated for thousands of years. Long before the Spanish established colonies in the Americas, the native Americans made mild alcoholic drinks from yuccas. However, while they extracted from them everything from soap to food, they tended not to use them in an ornamental context.

Soon after they arrived, the Spanish began sending plant specimens back to Europe. Most species flourished in the Mediterranean climate and, thankfully, many yuccas also grew well in temperate climates as the cold desert nights of their natural habitat had toughened them up, enabling them to cope with very low temperatures. However, good drainage and a sunny location are required for most yuccas growing in temperate climates.

Yuccas are evergreens. Some, including *Yucca filamontosa*, never form a trunk; the mature part of the plant dies after flowering but the remaining offsets live on. Others, such as *Yucca recurvifolia*, form trunks which branch after flowering, and a few, such as *Yucca glauca*, form a single, short trunk that lives on after flowering.

The many species available offer a great variety of shapes and colours so that, whether used as specimen plants in containers or as part of mixed plantings, there is always the opportunity to make a strong architectural impact with them. Most yuccas have white, bell-shaped flowers, sometimes tinged with red or purple. They form impressive flowering spikes which last for many weeks. In cool climates these spikes can flower out of sequence. This is because the summer heat is inadequate to make them flower in one year. In a hotter climate the flowers would bloom in early summer but in a cool climate, flower spikes do not always open until later in the growing season. Some of the varieties are mildly scented.

## PERSONAL FAVOURITES

Y. *gloriosa* 'Variegata' (single-stemmed)

Y. *filamentosa* (clumping)

Y. *rostrata* (blue foliage)

## *Yucca aloifolia* – Spanish bayonet

A distinctive yucca, cultivated since 1605

**Cold-hardiness**
To -18°C (0°F)

**Growth rate in temperate climates**
Medium

**Commercial availability**
Mediocre to good

**Cultural requirements**
Prefers full sun best but tolerates some shade, in fast-draining soil

**Cold-weather protection**
Provide increasing protection, with fleece and then hay, when temperatures drop below -6°C (25°F)

**Leaf**
Sharp and green; the cultivar 'Marginata' has either a yellow or a white margin and 'Tricolour' has either a yellow or a white medial stripe

**Trunk**
Single-stemmed; occasional branching, mainly from the base

**Flower stalk**
The stem, up to 50cm (1ft 4in) long, carries white flowers which sometimes have a purple or green hue

**Propagation**
By removal of offsets and germination of seeds in the spring, in temperatures from 17–27°C (31–80°F). Propagation from stem and root cuttings is also possible

**Origin**
USA, Mexico

*Yucca aloifolia* 'Variegata'

# *Yucca filamentosa* (*Variegata* shown below) – Adam's needle

A useful, small yucca, the leaves have unusual filaments and are not sharp

**Cold-hardiness**
To -29°C (-20°F)

**Growth rate in temperate climates**
Medium to fast

**Commercial availability**
Good

**Cultural requirements**
Prefers sun but will grow in partial shade in fast-draining, reasonably fertile soil

**Cold-weather protection**
Cover younger specimens with straw when temperatures drop below -6°C (21°F)

**Leaf**
Green to glaucous in colour, flaccid and lance-shaped

**Trunk**
No trunk; grows in clumps up to 50cm (1ft 4in) across

**Flower stalk**
These can reach up to 4m (13ft) in their native environment; they carry creamy-white flowers sometimes tinged with pink

**Propagation**
By removal of offsets and germination of seeds in spring, in temperatures of 17–27°C (31–80°F)

**Origin**
USA

# Yucca flaccida – (No common name)

A useful, small yucca, the leaves have unusual filaments and are not sharp

**Cold-hardiness**
To -29°C (-20°F)

**Growth rate in temperate climates**
Medium to fast

**Commercial availability**
Good

**Cultural requirements**
Prefers sun but will grow in partial shade in fast-draining, reasonably fertile soil

**Cold-weather protection**
Will tolerate damp soil in winter but cover younger specimens with straw when temperatures drop below -6°C (21°F)

**Leaf**
Green, flaccid and lance-shaped; the cultivar 'Glaucescens' has a wider, more erect and glaucous leaf, 'Ivory' has grey-green leaves with creamy variegation, and 'Lineata' has yellow stripes that fade with time

**Trunk**
No trunk; grows in clumps up to 70cm (2ft 3in) in height

**Flower stalk**
Can reach up to 2m (6ft 6in), with creamy, lightly fragrant flowers

**Propagation**
By removal of offsets and germination of seeds in spring, in temperatures from 17–27°C (31–80°F)

**Origin**
USA

*Yucca flaccida* 'Gold Sword'

# *Yucca gloriosa* – Spanish dagger

A good value, common species

**Cold-hardiness**
To -7°C (19°F)

**Growth rate in temperate climates**
Medium to fast

**Commercial availability**
Good

**Cultural requirements**
Soil with good drainage. Prefers full sun; while it will grow in partial shade, variegated varieties lose much of their variegation

**Cold-weather protection**
Provide increasing protection, by encasing in straw and keeping the roots dry, when temperatures drop below -6°C (21°F)

**Leaf**
Green, soft and fairly wide; the cultivar 'Medio Picta' is variegated

**Trunk**
Single and multi-stemmed, it can reach up to 4.6m (15ft)

**Flower stalk**
Can reach up to 1.2m (3ft 10in), with white flowers that are sometimes suffused with purple or red

**Propagation**
By removal of offsets and germination of seeds in spring, in temperatures of 17–27°C (31–80°F); propagation from stem cuttings is also possible

**Origin**
USA

*Yucca gloriosa* 'Variegata'

## *Yucca rostrata* – Beaked yucca

A beautiful blue species

**Cold-hardiness**
To -13°C (9°F)

**Growth rate in temperate climates**
Medium

**Commercial availability**
Mediocre to good

**Cultural requirements**
Prefers full sun but tolerates light shade, in fast-draining soil

**Cold-weather protection**
Cover younger specimens with straw when temperatures drop below -6°C (21°F)

**Leaf**
Thin and light blue

**Trunk**
Single, can reach up to 2m (6ft 6in)

**Flower stalk**
Can reach up to 60cm (2ft), with white flowers

**Propagation**
Germination of seeds in spring, in temperatures of 17–27°C (31–80°F)

**Origin**
USA and Mexico

# Yucca whipplei – Our Lord's candle

An attractive species, resistant to salty winds

**Cold-hardiness**
To -12°C (10°F)

**Growth rate in temperate climates**
Moderate

**Commercial availability**
Mediocre to good

**Cultural requirements**
Fast-draining soil in a sunny position

**Cold-weather protection**
Provide increasing protection when
temperatures drop below -6°C (21°F)

**Leaf**
Bluey-green, sharp and thin

**Trunk**
No trunk; grows in clumps up to 2m
(6ft 6in)

**Flower stalk**
Can reach up to 4m (13ft), with white
flowers

**Propagation**
By removal of offsets or germination of
seeds in spring

**Origin**
USA

The impressive flower stalk
of a *Yucca whipplei*

# CHAPTER ELEVEN

# AGAVES

As with yuccas, the pulp of agaves has been used to make alcoholic beverages for thousands of years – tequila is the most well known today. Their leaves are also used to make fibres used for weaving coarse fabrics, and extracts from agave roots and stems have been used to make laxatives and soaps.

Fantastically exotic, these succulents require sunny positions and good drainage. When siting, consideration must be given to their sharp leaf ends: these make the plants difficult to move without sustaining cuts and scratches. When specimens are moved, the leaves tear very easily and tend to break off if they catch against anything hard. Wipe damaged leaves with fungicide and leave them to dry: their ends become much thinner and quite crisp. Prune them back to dry side of the point at which the live part meets the dry part.

If agaves are exposed to excessively cold temperatures, their leaves become translucent and then die. By keeping the roots dry and providing heavy protection against cold and damp weather, you will be able to grow good specimens.

As it takes so long for many agaves to flower, they tend to be grown mainly for their foliage. Smaller species can flower within eight years, but without the impact of flower spires that reach 7m (23ft).

## PERSONAL FAVOURITES

*A. americana*

*A. parryi*

*A. utahensis*

A terraced garden with rows of palms and agaves

The green foliage of the palms and ferns highlights the grey of the agaves

This mixed planting of agaves shows the wide range of colours available

## *Agave americana* – Century plant

One of the best-value agaves due to its rapid growth and reasonable price

**Cold-hardiness**
Green, to -9°C (16°F); variegated, to -4°C (25°F)

**Growth rate in temperate climates**
Moderate to fast

**Commercial availability**
Good

**Cultural requirements**
Free-draining soil with sun for at least half the day, preferably more

**Cold-weather protection**
Keep the roots dry and provide increasing protection for variegated forms when temperatures drop below -1°C (30°F) and for green forms when they drop below -3°C (27°F)

**Leaf**
The hard-pointed, green to glaucous leaves form rosettes and can reach up to 2m (6ft 6in) in length in old specimens. The cultivar 'Marginata' has stripes of yellow or white on the leaf margins, 'Mediopicta' has a yellow or white longitudinal stripe

**Trunk**
No trunk – forms massive rosettes

**Flower stalk**
Can reach up to 8m (26ft), with yellow flowers

**Propagation**
Generally through the removal of offsets

**Origin**
Mexico

## *Agave neomexicana* – Mescal

An attractive, uniform species

**Cold-hardiness**
To -29°C (-20°F)

**Growth rate in temperate climates**
Slow to moderate

**Commercial availability**
Poor to mediocre

**Cultural requirements**
In full sun and soil with very good drainage

**Cold-weather protection**
Keep roots dry and provide increasing protection
when temperatures drop below -5°C (23°F)

**Leaf**
Green to glaucous-grey

**Trunk**
No trunk – readily forms rosettes

**Flower stalk**
Can reach up to 3.5m (11ft 6in), with yellow
flowers

**Propagation**
By germination of seeds in spring at a
temperature of around 21°C (70°F) or removal
of offsets

**Origin**
USA

## *Agave parryi* – (No common name)

A very cold-hardy agave

**Cold-hardiness**
To -29°C (-20°F)

**Growth rate in temperate climates**
Slow to moderate

**Commercial availability**
Mediocre to good

**Cultural requirements**
Fast-draining soil in full sun

**Cold-weather protection**
Keep roots dry and provide increasing protection
when temperatures drop below -6°C (21°F)

**Leaf**
Glaucous-grey and spiky

**Trunk**
No trunk – sometimes forms a single rosette,
usually produces groups of offsets

**Flower stalk**
Can reach up to 6m (19ft 6in), with yellow flowers

**Propagation**
By germination of seeds in spring at a
temperature of around 21°C (70°F) or removal
of offsets

**Origin**
USA and Mexico

# *Agave utahensis* – (No common name)

A small, variable agave

**Cold-hardiness**
To -18°C (0°F), but varies according to variety

**Growth rate in temperate climates**
Slow to moderate

**Commercial availability**
Poor to mediocre

**Cultural requirements**
Full sun and exceptionally good drainage

**Cold-weather protection**
Keep roots bone dry and provide increasing protection when temperatures drop below -5°C (23°F)

**Leaf**
Green-grey

**Trunk**
No trunk; usually forms a sizeable clump

**Flower stalk**
Can reach up to 2.5m (8ft), with yellow flowers

**Propagation**
By germination of seeds in spring at a temperature of around 21°C (70°F) or removal of offsets

**Origin**
USA

# CHAPTER TWELVE

# CORDYLINES

Cordylines are often mistaken for palms. In fact, their nickname is 'Torbay palm', from the seaside town of Torbay in the south-west of England, where they line the main streets. Most of the frost-hardy species are native to New Zealand while the less hardy types, such as *Cordyline fruticosa*, come from tropical Southeast Asia; these could be used in planters or even summer bedding schemes.

The most common hardy cordyline is *Cordyline australis*. With all species, green varieties tend to be the most hardy. I have seen specimens around London with trunks of at least 35cm (just over 1ft) in diameter and up to 5m (16ft 6in) tall. As with hardy palms, the trunks of hardy cordylines become much thicker in a temperate climate when they are grown from small specimens. It is possible to purchase specimens up to 4m (13ft) tall but, because they have invariably been grown in a warmer climate, their trunks are usually half the thickness of those grown from small specimens in a cooler climate. Also, as the leaves of imported plants are softer, they must be protected from hard frost until they thicken up. For example, locally grown, mature specimens could tolerate temperatures as low as -10°C (14°F) whereas imported plants might only survive down to -5°C (23°F) until they become acclimatized.

The lance-shaped leaves of cordylines complement palm leaves well, and they come in a wide range of colours. Green-leaved plants are the hardiest, followed by red-leaved varieties, and variegated forms are the least hardy. Providing frost protection will help to develop the most attractive leaves.

Take care not to disturb a cordyline's roots unduly as they dislike being moved once they are established, and it is important that they have adequate anchorage so as to avoid wind rock. As cordylines are top-heavy, they are particularly prone to damage from wind rock. In light soils, if the trunk is unstable, place two paving stones on either side to hold it steady and help it root well.

The top growth of young cordylines is sometimes burnt back by frosts but they usually regenerate and produce multiple trunks, sometimes as many as six. This can look very attractive; green varieties that have developed in this way remind me of palms in an oasis. If you want a multi-stemmed specimen, cut off the top of the plant and treat the cut with a fungicide to guard against infection. This is best done as soon as the risk of frost has passed, leaving the plant the maximum time to grow before the onset of the next winter.

An increasingly popular alternative to *Cordyline australis* is the wider-leafed *C. indivisa*, which has both a green and a purple form. Aptly named, it will not divide as readily as *C. australis* – 'indivisa' means single trunk.

When grown from small specimens in a temperate climate, cordylines will develop thick trunks

When cordyline trunks are damaged, they will often regenerate and divide at the top

A *Cordyline australis* with multiple trunks, dividing from the base

## CORDYLINE HYBRIDS

These hybrids are all of uncertain parentage

*Cordyline* 'Autumn Bronze'
Red leaves with gold edges; it can reach up to 4m (13ft)

*Cordyline* 'Emerald Isle'
Green foliage: this plant is hardy to -7°C (19°F)

*Cordyline* 'Pink Stripe'
A slow-growing plant with thin leaves, this can reach up to 3m (10ft); it is best grown in a sheltered position where it can be kept well protected

*Cordyline* 'Ti Tahiti'
Hardy to -3°C (27°F), this plant can reach up to 4m (13ft)

*Cordyline* 'Pink Stripe'

## OTHER INTERESTING CORDYLINES

*Cordyline banksii*
A multi-trunked plant with light green leaves, hardy to -4°C (25°F). There is also a purple form

*Cordyline pumilio*
This grass-like species requires largely frost-free conditions and reaches only up to 1m (3ft 3in)

*Cordyline* 'Red Fountain'
This cross between *C. pumilio* and *C. banksii* has a purple leaf and is phormium-like in appearance

## PERSONAL FAVOURITES

*C. australis* 'Albertii' (variegated)
*C. australis* 'Red Star' (bronze-red)
*C. indivisa* (green)

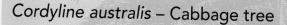

# *Cordyline australis* – Cabbage tree

This species grows well and looks good both in pots and in the ground

### Cold-hardiness
The degree of hardiness varies depending on foliage colour and cultivar

Green foliage, to -9°C (16°F)

'Sundance' (green with red central vein), to -6°C (21°F)

'Torbay Dazzler' (variegated), to -6°C (21°F)

'Albertii' (variegated), to -6°C (21°F)

'Variegata' (variegated), to -7°C (19°F)

'Karo Kiri' (green-yellow mid-rib), to -6°C (21°F)

Purpurea Group (light purple), to -5°C (23°F)

'Purple Tower' (deep purple), to -6°C (21°F)

'Red Star' (bronze-red), to -7°C (19°F)

### Growth rate in temperate climates
Medium; green varieties are the fastest

### Commercial availability
Very good to mediocre, according to cultivar

### Cultural requirements
Well-drained soil in sunny position; green plants require the least sun and will grow when there is sun for only one-third of the day, red plants require sun for half the day and variegated plants for two-thirds of the day

### Cold-weather protection
The degree of cold against which protection is required depends upon the colour and size of the plant. Move pot-grown plants to a more sheltered environment, and draw and tie the leaves of both pot and ground plants together. In particularly harsh weather, encase in straw. Keep roots on the dry side during the winter

### Leaf
Narrow and sword-like; colour varies according to cultivar (see entry for 'Cold-hardiness')

### Trunk
Single- and multiple-stemmed

### Fruits
White or blue

### Flower stalk
Can reach up to 1m (3ft 3in), with long, creamy flowers

### Propagation
Sow seeds in spring, at 17°C (31°F). Well-established basal suckers can be cut off in the spring. Cultivars are propagated by root cuttings

### Origin
New Zealand

## *Cordyline indivisa* – Mountain cabbage tree

A challenging but rewarding cordyline

**Cold-hardiness**
To -8°C (17°F)

**Growth rate in temperate climates**
Medium

**Commercial availability**
Mediocre

**Cultural requirements**
Well-drained but damp, moisture-holding soil in partial to full shade

**Cold-weather protection**
Draw and tie leaves together when temperatures drop below -5°C (23°F)

**Leaf**
Narrow and sword-like; green and purple forms have an orange mid-rib

**Trunk**
Single, can reach up to 3m (10ft)

**Flower stalk**
Can reach up to 1.5m (5ft), with creamy flowers

**Fruit**
Purple-blue berries

**Propagation**
Sow seeds in spring at 17°C (31°F)

**Origin**
New Zealand

## *Cordyline kaspar* – Three Kings cabbage tree

Named after one of the Three Kings Islands, a group of 13 islands off the northern tip of New Zealand, this is a shorter and fatter-leafed cordyline than *C. australis*.

**Cold-hardiness**
To -6°C (21°F)

**Growth rate in temperate climates**
Moderate

**Commercial availability**
Mediocre

**Cultural requirements**
Well-drained, sunny location

**Cold-weather protection**
Either grow in a pot and move to a sheltered position in harsh weather or draw and tie the leaves together and encase in straw, and keep the roots dry

**Leaf**
Either green or bronze, wide and sword-like, they can reach up to 60cm (24in) in length

**Trunk**
Multi-branched, can reach up to 4m (13ft); 'Green Goddess' is a little shorter, reaching up to 3m (10ft)

**Fruit**
Purple

**Flower stalk**
Can reach up to 1m (3ft 3in) in length, with white, fragrant flowers

**Propagation**
Sow seeds in spring at 17°C (31°F)

**Origin**
Three Kings Islands, off the north coast of New Zealand

# CHAPTER THIRTEEN

# PHORMIUMS AND ASTELIAS

I have grouped phormiums and astelias together as they share a number of characteristics – they are both evergreen and happiest in fast-draining soils – and are similar in appearance, with their long, sword-shaped leaves.

## PHORMIUMS

Phormiums, native to New Zealand, are evergreen flaxes with sword-shaped leaves. Most species are hardy in temperate climates. Although they can survive in colder regions, they do benefit from very careful siting (see Cultural requirements on p 139.) and some protection in harsh weather. Cultivars vary in height from 40cm to 3m (1ft 3in to 10ft).

Phormiums prefer a well-drained soil. This is critical in frosty conditions as wet roots will rot when they freeze. If you have heavy soil, incorporating plenty of grit and humus in the planting hole will help. They generally don't grow well in hot climates but seem to grow well near the sea, probably because the temperatures in such areas tend to be milder.

Dramatic, arching plants, they come in a wide range of colours. *Phormium tenax* and *P. cookianum* have been hybridized to produce dozens of plants of differing size and colour. While their orange or yellow flowers are not showy, they do add spring and summer interest and the subsequent seed pods are attractive in winter.

*Phormium tenax* has erect leaves that can reach up to 3m (10ft) in length and, a bonus for urban gardeners, will tolerate air pollution. The leaves of *P. cookianum* can reach up to 1.5m (5ft) in length and are weeping in nature; hybrid leaves tend to be either erect or weeping. When propagating by division, leaves can be cut back by two-thirds to reduce root rock if a wind-free location is unavailable.

In harsh weather a coarse mulch will help protect the plant, but this should be removed as temperatures rise to avoid its base rotting.

## PERSONAL FAVOURITES

*P.* 'Maori Sunrise'
*P.* 'Mahogany'
*P.* 'Yellow Wave'

*Phormium* 'Variegatum'

*Phormium* 'Platt's Black'

*Phormium* subsp. *hookeri*
'Cream Delight'

*Phormium* 'Jester'

# Phormium species – (New Zealand flax)

Attractive, evergreen flaxes with sword-shaped leaves

**Cold-hardiness**
To -10°C (14°F)

**Growth rate in temperate climates**
Fast

**Commercial availability**
Good

**Cultural requirements**
Well-drained soil that is dry in winter but a little damper in summer, in sun for at least half the day

**Cold-weather protection**
Wrap well in fleece in harsh weather. Pot specimens can be moved to a warmer location: in winter, a cold, damp, shady location can kill these plants

**Leaf**
Sword-like in shape, the leaf varies in length from less than 1m to 2.5m (3ft 3in to 8ft). Some varieties are erect, others are weeping in habit

**Trunk**
No trunk

**Flower stalk**
Can reach up to 3m (10ft), according to variety, with orange flowers

**Fruit**
The dry seed-heads are unusual in appearance – up to 30cm (1ft) long and black

**Propagation**
By sowing seeds in the spring at temperatures of around 18°C (0°F), or division, again in the spring

**Origin**
New Zealand

# ASTELIAS

These evergreen perennials grow in damp conditions in New Zealand. In time they form large arching clumps. While most astelias are not sufficiently frost-hardy to grow outside, if they are sited carefully and provided with protection when temperatures drop much below -3°C (27°F), they can cope with a temperate climate.

*Astelia nervosa*

Like phormiums, astelias do not like being moved around so care is required when dividing for propagation purposes. Generally, the smaller the offset the greater the chance of it doing well. Even though it is said to like moist conditions, this is not true when growing in frosty conditions, because of damage to the roots. Astelias are happiest in fast-draining soil that is kept on the dry side if temperatures drop below 0°C (32°F). I let mine dry out before watering them again, as they seem to rot around the base very easily.

One of the most exotic varieties is *Astelia chathamica* 'Silver Spear'. This has wide, arching, silver leaves that can reach up to 2m (6ft 6in) in length. The yellow-green flowers are followed by orange berries. There are a number of rare forms of this astelia with a prominent red mid-rib. *Astelia nervosa*, reputed to be more hardy than *A. c.* 'Silver Spear', can reach up to 1.7m (5ft 6in). It has silvery-green leaves, thinner than those of *A. c.* 'Silver Spear'. *Astelia solandri* is similar in colour to *A. c.* 'Silver Spear' but, again, has a thinner leaf. All can take considerably more shade than phormiums.

*Astelia nervosa* 'Westland'

## PERSONAL FAVOURITES

*A. chathamica* 'Silver Spear'
*A. nervosa* 'Westland'

# *Astelia species* – (No general common name)

Attractive, evergreen perennials with a flax-like appearance

**Cold-hardiness**
To -6°C (21°F) according to variety;
*A. chathamica* and *A. nervosa* are
the hardiest types

**Growth rate in temperate climates**
Moderate

**Commercial availability**
Mediocre to good

**Cultural requirements**
A sheltered position with well-drained soil.
Both *A. chathamica* and *A. nervosa* cope
with considerable shade

**Cold-weather protection**
Wrap in fleece in harsh weather

**Leaf**
Sword-like in shape, the length varies from
50cm to 2m (1ft 4in to 6ft 6in) according
to variety, and the colour may be green,
silver or silver suffused with red

**Trunk**
No trunk

**Flower stalk**
Can reach up to 40cm (1ft 3in), with
orange flowers

**Fruit**
Orange berries

**Propagation**
By division of clumps in the spring; seeds
can be sown in cold frames once ripe

**Origin**
New Zealand

*Astelia chathamica* 'Silver Spear'

*Astelia grandis*

# CHAPTER FOURTEEN

# MISCELLANEOUS SPIKY PLANTS

This selection will allow you to further expand your collection of hardy palm-like plants. Herbaceous plants, such as *Eryngium* spp., can be cheap and useful fillers. However, as they get bigger — up to 2m (6ft 6in) in height — they can become a bit untidy. Some evergreen *Carex* varieties, including 'Evergold', complement small palms well. Variegated irises have strong leaf shapes that overwinter well in mild locations. The herbaceous *Aciphylla* spp. include varieties that mimic yuccas and they can look very imposing. Just look around and you will find other plants with linear leaves that work well with the plants listed in this Directory.

## *Beschorneria yuccoides* – Mexican lily

An attractive yucca lookalike

**Cold-hardiness**
To -8°C (17°F)

**Growth rate in temperate climates**
Moderate

**Commercial availability**
Mediocre to good

**Cultural requirements**
Fast-draining, organically rich soil

**Cold-weather protection**
Keep roots dry and provide increasing protection when temperatures drop below -3°C (27°F)

**Leaf**
Green to glaucous

**Trunk**
No trunk; develops clump-forming rosettes which can reach up to 1.7m (5ft 6in)

**Flower stalks**
Can reach up to 1.2m (3ft 10in), with red flowers

**Propagation**
By removal of offsets or sowing of seeds in spring, at a temperature of around 21°C (70°F)

**Origin**
Mexico

# *Cycas panzhihuaensis* – Sago palm

New introduction from China, reputed to be the fastest-growing and hardiest cycad

**Cold-hardiness**
To -8°C (17°F)

**Growth rate in temperate climates**
Slow

**Commercial availability**
Mediocre

**Cultural requirements**
Free-draining soil in a sunny position

**Cold-weather protection**
Either grow in a pot that can be moved to a more sheltered location in winter or plant outside in a very sheltered position

**Leaf**
Pinnate and green

**Trunk**
1 to 2m (6ft 6in)

**Flower stalk**
Up to 40cm (1ft 3in), with yellow flowers

**Propagation**
Sow seeds in spring during periods when temperatures are between 15° and 28°C (59° and 82°F)

**Origin**
China

# Cycas revoluta – Sago palm

The most common cycad; even small specimens look imposing

**Cold-hardiness**
To -5°C (23°F)

**Growth rate in temperate climates**
Slow

**Commercial availability**
Good

**Cultural requirements**
Free-draining soil in a sunny position

**Cold-weather protection**
Either grow in a pot that can be moved to a more sheltered location in winter or plant outside in a very sheltered position. Provide increasing protection when temperatures drop below -3°C (27°F)

**Leaf**
Dark green

**Trunk**
Multi-stemmed, can reach up to 3m (10ft)

**Flower stalk**
None

**Propagation**
Sow seeds in spring during periods when temperatures are between 15° and 28°C (59° and 82°F)

**Origin**
Japan

## *Dasylirion wheeleri* – Desert spoon

An attractive plant for pot culture

**Cold-hardiness**
To -18°C (0°F), though generally much lower in temperate climates

**Growth rate in temperate climates**
Slow to moderate

**Commercial availability**
Mediocre

**Cultural requirements**
Free-draining soil in sunny location

**Cold-weather protection**
Keep roots dry in winter and provide increasing protection when temperatures drop below -3°C (27°F)

**Leaf**
Glaucous to blue

**Trunk**
Can reach up to 1.5m (5ft)

**Flower stalks**
Can reach up to 6m (20ft), with tall, white flowers

**Propagation**
Sowing of seeds in spring, at a temperature of around 21°C (70°F)

**Origin**
USA and Mexico

# *Fascicularia bicolor* – (No common name)

Stunning, red-centred bromeliad

**Cold-hardiness**
To 0°C (32°F)

**Growth rate in temperate climates**
Medium

**Commercial availability**
Mediocre

**Cultural requirements**
Fast-draining position in full sun

**Cold-weather protection**
Keep roots dry in winter and provide increasing protection when temperatures drop below -2°C (28°F)

**Leaf**
Green with red centres

**Trunk**
No trunk; forms rosettes

**Flower stalks**
Can reach up to 20cm (8in), with blue flowers

**Propagation**
By removal of offsets or sowing of seeds in spring at a temperature of around 20°C (68°F)

**Origin**
Chile

The red-centred leaves of
*Fascicularia bicolor*

## *Furcraea foetida* – Mediterranean hemp

This variegated plant needs a virtually frost-free climate, but it is spectacularly exotic

**Cold-hardiness**
To 0˚C (32˚F)

**Growth rate in temperate climates**
Medium

**Commercial availability**
Mediocre

**Cultural requirements**
Organically rich, fast-draining soil in a sunny location

**Cold-weather protection**
Best grown in a pot so that it can be moved to a frost-free environment in cold weather

**Leaf**
Green or variegated (*F. f.* 'Variegata' and *F. f.* var. *mediopicta* are both variegated plants)

**Trunk**
No trunk

**Flower stalks**
Can reach up to 2.4m (7ft 10in)

**Propagation**
By removal of offsets or stem bulbils

**Origin**
South America

# *Puya chilensis* – (No common name)

An exotic-looking bromeliad

**Cold-hardiness**
To -5°C (23°F)

**Growth rate in temperate climates**
Moderate

**Commercial availability**
Mediocre to good

**Cultural requirements**
Fast-draining soil in full sun

**Cold-weather protection**
Keep roots dry in winter and provide increasing protection when temperatures drop below -2°C (28°F)

**Leaf**
Green to glaucous

**Trunk**
No trunk; rosette-forming

**Flower stalk**
Can reach up to 1.5m (5ft), with yellow-green flowers

**Propagation**
Seeds germinate at temperatures around 20–24°C (68–75°F)

**Origin**
Chile

# CHAPTER FIFTEEN

# INDOOR PLANTS

While the main aim of this book is to explore palms and spiky plants that grow well in a temperate climate, many people like to use them as indoor plants. Since Victorian times, when parlour palms were in vogue, the range of palms available for use as indoor plants has steadily increased.

Some palms, such as *Rhapis excelsa* and *Howea forsteriana*, make excellent indoor plants. They only grow slowly but they can tolerate dark corners; while indirect light may make them grow a little faster, direct light could burn their foliage. Variegated forms of *R. excelsa* grow best in very low light levels. Areca palms are cheaper than Rhapis or Howea but need higher light levels.

Many chamaedoreas, *C. metallica* in particular, make excellent low-light, indoor plants. The most common indoor yucca is *Y. elephantipes*, but it needs fairly high levels of light to grow well.

A number of outdoor palms could grow happily in a conservatory but avoid those that originate from a temperate climate, including *Trachycarpus* spp. While *Phoenix canariensis* are good value, their prickly leaves might be a problem when they get bigger; *P. roebelenii*, the dwarf date palm, is a safer choice. Other palms worth trying are *Livistona*, *Dypsis*, *Caryota* and *Washingtonia* spp.

Cordylines, dracaenas and agaves would also be at home in your conservatory though the common *A. americana* might become too big within a few years; some of the smaller agaves would be better for the long term. Cycads, although slow growing, would offer an interesting foliage alternative.

You could try many of the miscellaneous spiky plants listed in the previous chapter; *Beschorneria yuccoides* and *Furcraea* spp. make good house plants. Over time, puyas grow too big.

## PERSONAL FAVOURITES

*Howea forsteriana*
*Rhapis excelsa*
*Yucca elephantipes*

*Growing indoors on the larger scale: the palm house in Birmingham Botanical Gardens in England*

## *Areca species* – (No general common name)

These are relatively cheap plants, but they need to be kept near a window

**Growth rate in temperate climates**
Slow to medium

**Commercial availability**
Good

**Cultural requirements**
Use a slow-release fertilizer, and water when compost dries out

**Leaf**
Pinnate and green

**Trunk**
Clumping

**Flower stalk**
Can reach up to 1m (3ft 3in), with yellow flowers

**Fruit**
Yellow to red

**Propagation**
Fresh seed germinates within 12 weeks and benefits from heating under the compost tray

**Origin**
Southeast Asia

## *Chamaedorea elegans* – Parlour palm

Tolerates light frost, so can also be used outside

**Growth rate in temperate climates**
Slow to medium

**Commercial availability**
Good

**Cultural requirements**
Use a slow-release fertilizer, and water when compost dries out

**Leaf**
Pinnate and green

**Trunk**
Clumping

**Flower stalk**
Can reach up to 60cm (2ft), with yellow flowers

**Fruit**
Black

**Propagation**
Production of fresh seed is erratic and germination can take up to one year

**Origin**
Mexico

# *Howea forsteriana* – Kentia palm

One of the best shade-tolerant, indoor palms, this plant copes with considerable neglect

**Cold-hardiness**
Could be used outside in a largely shady position as it can take a few degrees of frost; to -3°C (27°F) when mature

**Growth rate in temperate climates**
Slow to medium

**Commercial availability**
Very good

**Cultural requirements**
Use a slow-release fertilizer, and water when compost dries out. Indoor specimens benefit from being placed outside in warm weather periodically

**Leaf**
Pinnate and green

**Trunk**
Solitary

**Flower stalk**
Can reach up to 1m (3ft 3in), with green (female) or light brown (male) flowers

**Fruit**
Yellow to red

**Propagation**
Germination of seeds is erratic and may take up to two years

**Origin**
Lord Howe Island, off the east coast of Australia

## *Phoenix roebelenii* – Dwarf date palm

Tolerates lower light levels than most *Phoenix* spp. and can be placed outside in a tub during frost-free periods

**Growth rate in temperate climates**
Moderate

**Commercial availability**
Good

**Cultural requirements**
Humus-rich, well-fed soil in a bright location, preferably with indirect light. Water during dry periods

**Cold-weather protection**
If used outside, move to a frost-free position before the first frost arrives

**Leaf**
Green

**Trunk**
Solitary and clumping, can reach up to 2m (6ft 6in)

**Flower stalk**
Can reach up to 70cm (2ft 3in), with creamy flowers

**Fruit**
Black

**Propagation**
Seeds usually germinate within three months

**Origin**
Laos

## *Yucca elephantipes* – Giant yucca

The most common form of indoor yucca

**Cold-hardiness**
To -3°C (27°F); I have overwintered mine on an unprotected porch without a problem

**Growth rate in temperate climates**
Slow

**Commercial availability**
Very good

**Cultural requirements**
Requires watering every few weeks in the summer and every other month in the winter; keep near a window

**Leaf**
Green

**Trunk**
Branching, will reach the ceiling in time

**Flower stalk**
Can reach 4–5m (13ft to 16ft 6in) in the wild, less when grown indoors, with white flowers

**Propagation**
By stem cuttings

**Origin**
Mexico

# RESOURCES

SUPPLIERS

SOCIETIES

GARDENS

FURTHER READING

# SUPPLIERS

## SPECIMEN PLANTS

### United Kingdom

The Palm Centre
Ham Nursery
Ham Street
Ham
Richmond
Surrey TW10 7HA
Tel: 020 8255 6191
Fax: 020 8255 6192
email: mail@palmcentre.co.uk
www.palmcentre.co.uk
Widest selection of plants in
UK; palm paradise

The Palm Farm
Thornton Hall Gardens
Ullery
North Lincolnshire DN39 6XF
Tel: 01469 531232
Modest selection of plants

Burncoose Nurseries
Gwennap
Redruth
Cornwall TR16 6BJ
Tel: 01209 860316/861112
Fax: 01209 860011
email:
burncoose@ecl.pse.co.uk
www.eclipse.co.uk/burncoose
Good selection of phormiums
and cordylines

Trevena Cross Nurseries
Breage
Helston
Cornwall TR13 9PS
Tel: 01736 763880
Fax: 01736 762828
Excellent selection of plants

Architectural Plants
Cooks Farm
Nuthurst
West Sussex RH13 6LH
Tel:01243 545772
Fax: 01403 891056
www.gardening-
uk.com/architecturalplants
Modest selection of plants

Abbotsbury Sub-Tropical
Gardens
Abbotsbury
Weymouth
Dorset DT3 4LA
Tel: 01305 871344
Modest selection of plants

Amulree Exotics
Katonia Avenue
Maylandsea
Essex CM3 6AD
(Nursery: Tropical Wings
Centre, Wickford, South
Woodham Ferrers, Essex CM3
5QZ)
Tel: 01621 744981
email:
sdg@exotica.fsbusiness.co.uk
Reasonably good selection of
plants

Drysdale Garden Exotics
Bowerwood Road
Fordingbridge
Hampshire SP6 1BN
Tel: 01425 653010
Modest selection of plants

P.J. Palms
41 Salcombe Road
Ashford, Middlesex TW15 3BS
Tel: 01784 250181
*Trachycarpus Wagnerianus*
specialist and modest range of
other plants

Rosedown Mill
Hartland, Bideford
Devon EX39 6AH
Tel: 01237 441527
www.rosedownmill.co.uk
Modest selection of plants

### United States

Brudys Exotics
PO Box 820874
Houston
TX 77282-0874
Tel: (713) 960 8887
www.brudys-exotics.com
Modest selection of plants

Neon Palm Nursery
3525 Stony Point Road
Santa Rosa
CA 95407
Tel: (707) 585 8100
Good selection of plants

Stokes Tropicals
PO Box 9868
4806 E. Old Spanish Trail
New Iberia, Los Angeles
CA 70562
Tel: (318) 365 6998
Modest selection of plants

K Van Vougondien & Sons
245 Route 109
PO Box 1000
Babylon
NY 11702
Tel: (800) 552 9996
Modest selection of plants

## SEEDS

### United Kingdom

The Palm Centre
(details given under Specimen
Plants)

Chiltern Seeds
Bortree Stile
Ulverston
Cumbria LA12 7PB
Tel: 1229 581137
Modest selection of seeds

### United States

Thompson & Morgan Inc.
PO Box 1308
Jackson
NJ 08527-0308
Tel: (800) 274 7333
Modest selection of seeds

# SOCIETIES

A good way to get information about palms is to search the Web. Society noticeboards can provide useful information about how plants perform locally. Many southern US states have their own societies and magazines. Their members can be a source of practical information, not only about what grows best, but also where to buy and see them locally. Details can be obtained from the website of the International Palm Society, which also has many links worth exploring.

## European Palm Society

Martin Gibbons
c/o The Palm Centre
Ham Central Nursery
Ham, Richmond,
Surrey, UK  TW10 7HA
email: Membership@palmsociety.org
Publishes the quarterly magazine *Chamaerops*, and organizes visits to exotic gardens

## International Palm Society

PO Box 1897
Lawrence
KS 66044-8897
www.palms.org
Publishes the quarterly magazine *Palms*, and organizes visits to gardens

## Local chapters of the International Palm Society

**Palm and Cycad Societies of Australia**
email: enquiries@pacsoa.org.au
www.pacsoa.org.au/index.html
Publishes *Principes Minor*, with five issues a year

**Palm and Cycad Societies of New Zealand**
email: palminfo@ihug.co.nz
Their magazine has four issues a year

**Pacific Northwest Palm and Exotic Plant Society**
email: via website
www.palms.org/pacific
Publishes excellent magazine for hardy exotics

**Fous de Palmier**
Manatte@libertysurf.fr
www.manureva.fr.st
Their magazine articles, written in French, emphasize hardy plants

**La Association Española de Amigos de las Palmeras**
email: Deborah@ctv.es
Publishes a quarterly magazine, in Spanish

# GARDENS

An excellent way to gather ideas for using palms and palm-like plants to best effect is to visit gardens that contain them. There are many beautiful gardens to visit in the US and in Europe. While some are laid out in palatial proportions, the interesting groupings can usually be reproduced on a smaller scale.

In Europe, the south of France, between Marseille and the Italian border, offers the greatest concentration of diversely planted gardens that are open to visitors. Travelling around this area, you can also see how people plant out their private gardens. In the US, the Huntington Gardens in California display a wide variety of plants.

## France

**Maria Serena**
Promenade Reine Astrid
Menton-Garavan
Tel: 04 92 10 33 66
The end of this garden forms the border with Italy. A modest number of different palms and spiky plants grow alongside an interesting mixture of trees, shrubs and other plants that grow around the villa

**Jardin Botanique Exotique Val Rahmeh**
Avenue St. Jaques
Menton-Garavan
Tel: 04 93 35 86 72
A lushly and heavily planted garden with many plants named. Miniature valleys have an almost jungle-like feel. A reasonable selection of palms and spiky plants can be seen growing alongside everything from large-leafed alocasias to temperate-climate shrubs

**Jardin Exotique-Zoo**
Pont d'Aran
Sanary-Bandol
Near Marseille
Tel: 9429 4038
Along with a zoo, this medium-sized garden has a modest selection of palms and spiky plants alongside other exotics

**Jardin Olbius Riquier**
Avenue Ambroise Thomas
Hyères
Tel: 04 94 57 48 99
This free garden has a good selection of mature palms and spiky plants laid out in a park

**Le Jardin Exotique d'Eze**
Eze
(between Nice and Monaco)
Tel: not available – written requests only
A few palm varieties and a modest collection of spiky plants grow alongside a wide variety of cacti and succulents

**Villa de Jardin Ephrussi Rothschild**
Saint Jean Cap Ferrat
Tel: 04 93 01 33 09
One of the more formal gardens has a palatial quality about it and a reasonable collection of palms and spiky plants

**Jardin Botanique de Villa-les-Cedres**
Saint Jean Cap Ferrat
Tel: not available – written requests only
This large garden has one of the best collections of palms and cycads on the Riviera. Entrance by application only; some genuine academic interest may need to be shown

**Parc Phoenix**
405 Promenade d'Anglais
Nice
Tel: 33 049321803
This park has a reasonable selection of plants and a huge greenhouse collection of tropical species

**Jardin Botanique Villa Thuret**
62 Boulevard du Cap
Cap d'Antibes
Antibes
Tel: 493 67 89 61
Excellent selection of palms and spiky plants grown in a mixed planting style

## Germany

**Wilhelma Gardens**
Neckartalstrasse
Stuttgart
Tel: 711 54020
Good collection of glasshouse palms

**Frankfurt Botanical Gardens**
Seismayerstrasse 72
Frankfurt
Tel: 069 798 2476
Good glasshouse collection

# Ireland

National Botanical Gardens
Glasnevin
Dublin
Tel: 8377596/8374388
Large palm house

# Italy

Botanical Garden and Arboretum 'Tor Vergata'
Largo Cristina di Svezia 24
Trastevere
Rome
Tel: 499 17107
Good palm collection

Botanical Garden of Naples
Bay Shore Drive 4820
Naples
Tel: 941 649 7306
Excellent palm and cycad collection

Giardini Botanici Hanbury
La Mortola
Ventimiglia
Italy
Tel: 0184 229507
Five minutes' drive from Menton, in France,
this large garden has a good agave collection.
A modest collection of spiky plants and palms
can be seen alongside a wide selection of
other plants, from cacti to eucalypts

# Monaco

Jardin Exotique de Monaco
62 Boulevard du Jardin Exotique
Tel: 377 93 15 29 80
Primarily a collection of cacti and spiky plants,
this garden also has a reasonable selection of
agaves and numerous succulents

# Netherlands

Botanical Gardens of Vrieje University
1105 De Boelelann
Amsterdam
Tel: 31 20 444 7777
Reasonable palm collection

# Portugal

Jardim Botânico
Rua da Escola Politécnica 56
Lisbon
Tel: 01 396 15 21
Good palm collection

# Spain

Jardi Botanic Mar i Murtra
Passeig Carles Faust 10
Blanes
Tel: 972 33 08 26
Many palms and succulents

Jardins Miramar
Mont Juic
Barcelona
Tel: 93 424 3809
Large palm garden

Jardin Botanico-Historico La Conception
Carretera de las Pedrizas
Near Malaga
Tel: 952 25 21 48
Over 150 years old and diversely planted, with
over 60 species of palm

# United Kingdom

Tresco Abbey Gardens
Tresco Estate
Tresco
Scilly Isles
Tel: 01720 4241052
The mild winters have allowed a wide variety of
plants to flourish

Royal Botanic Gardens, Kew
Richmond
Surrey
Tel: 020 8332 5000/5622
Excellent greenhouse specimens, limited
number of plants outside

Abbotsbury Subtropical Gardens
Bullers Way
Abbotsbury
Dorset
Tel: 01305 871387/871153
Good Mediterranean garden, many palms and
palm-like plants grown alongside a wide range
of other plants

The Lost Gardens of Heligan
Pentewan
St Austell
Cornwall
Tel: 01726 845100
Superb reclaimed Victorian garden using
modest numbers of palms and palm-like plants

Lamorran House Gardens
Upper Castle Road
St Mawes
Cornwall
Tel: 01326 270800
Wide variety of palms and palm-like plants
used in a normal garden setting

Trebah Gardens
Mawnan Smith
Near Falmouth
Cornwall
Tel: 01326 250448
This garden has mature Chusan palms and
many fine Mediterranean plants

## United States

Fairchild Tropical Garden
10901 Old Cutler Road
Miami
Florida
Tel: (305) 667 1651
World-class botanical gardens but limited
plants suitable for temperate gardens

Desert Botanical Garden
1201 North Galvin Parkway
Phoenix
Arizona
Tel: (480) 941-1225
Thirty-five types of yucca, 141 of agave

The Huntingdon Gardens
1151 Oxford Road
Los Angeles
California
Tel: 626 405 2100
Excellent collection of plants, with many
suitable for temperate climates

Harry P Leu Gardens
1920 N. Forest Avenue
Orlando
Florida
Tel: 407 246 2620
One of the best collections of palms and
cycads in Florida

The New York Botanical Garden
Bronx River Parkway and Fordham Road
The Bronx
New York
Tel: (718) 8178700
Good indoor palm collection

Bellevue Botanical Garden
12001 Main Street
Bellevue
Washington
Tel: (425) 4522750
Good palm collection

# FURTHER READING

Broschat and Meerow
*Ornamental Palm Horticulture*
University Press of Florida, US, 2000
In-depth guide to growing palms

Cave, Y and Paddison, V
*New Zealand Native Plants*
Timber Press, US, 2000
Cordylines, astelias and phormiums all
comprehensively described

Ellison, D
*Cultivated Palms of the World*
Briza Publications, South Africa, 2001
Well illustrated and comprehensive

Gibbons, M
*Identifying Palms*
Apple Press, UK, 1993
Good value, basic palm guide

Irish, M and G
*Agaves, Yuccas and Related Plants:
A Gardeners' Guide*
Timber Press, US, 2000
Agaves, yuccas and related plants all
comprehensively described

Jones, D
*Palms Throughout the World*
Reed Books, Australia, 1995
Excellent general book

# HARDINESS ZONES MAPS

## EUROPE

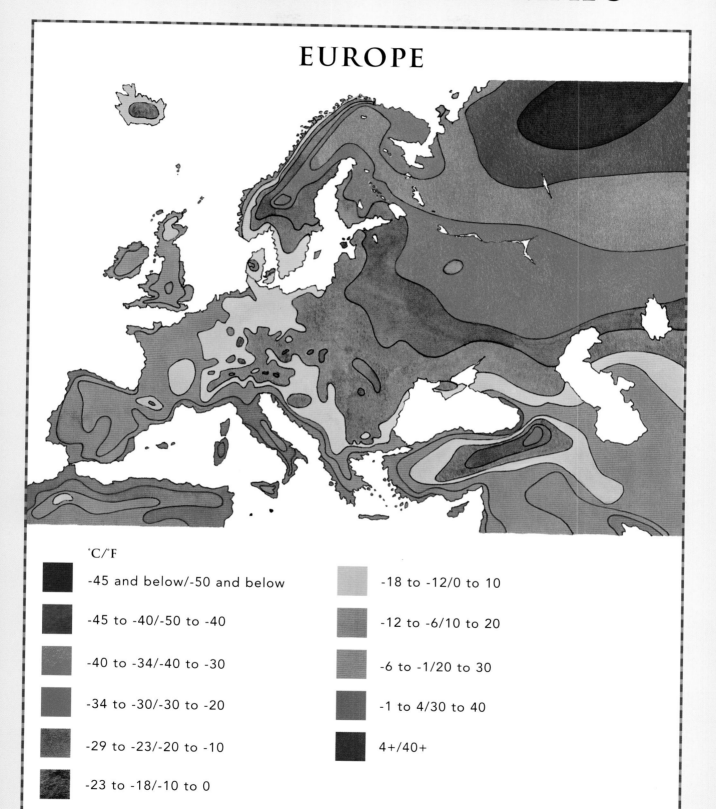

°C/°F

-45 and below/-50 and below

-45 to -40/-50 to -40

-40 to -34/-40 to -30

-34 to -30/-30 to -20

-29 to -23/-20 to -10

-23 to -18/-10 to 0

-18 to -12/0 to 10

-12 to -6/10 to 20

-6 to -1/20 to 30

-1 to 4/30 to 40

4+/40+

# USA

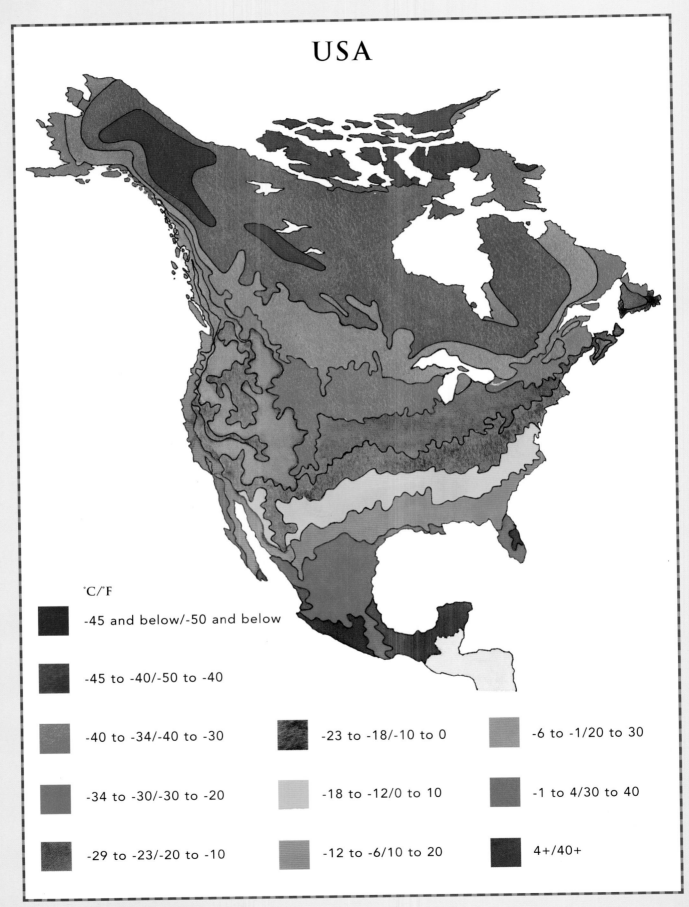

°C/°F

- -45 and below/-50 and below
- -45 to -40/-50 to -40
- -40 to -34/-40 to -30
- -34 to -30/-30 to -20
- -29 to -23/-20 to -10
- -23 to -18/-10 to 0
- -18 to -12/0 to 10
- -12 to -6/10 to 20
- -6 to -1/20 to 30
- -1 to 4/30 to 40
- 4+/40+

# NEW ZEALAND

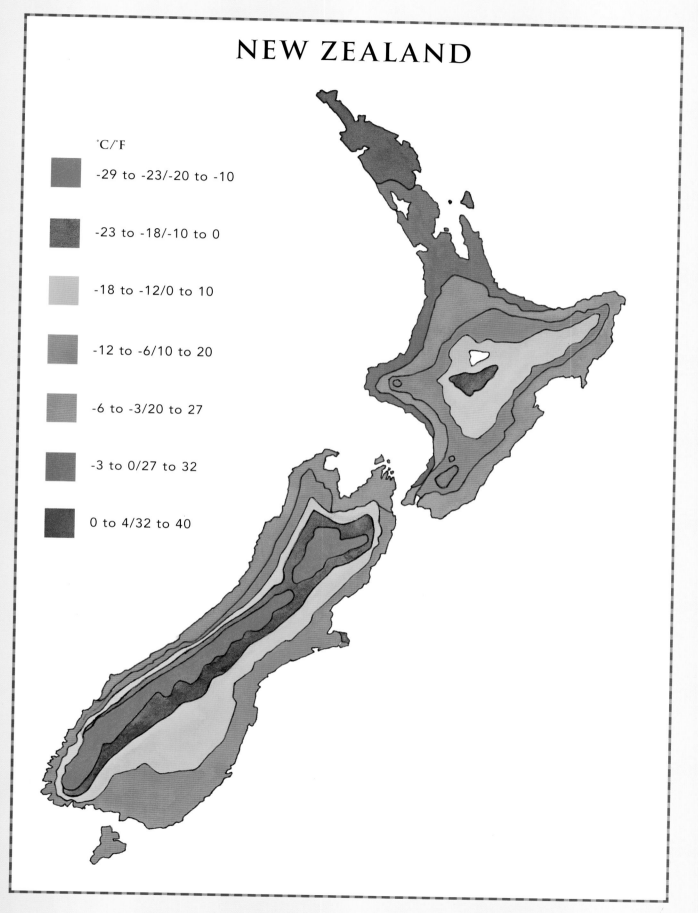

°C/°F

-29 to -23/-20 to -10

-23 to -18/-10 to 0

-18 to -12/0 to 10

-12 to -6/10 to 20

-6 to -3/20 to 27

-3 to 0/27 to 32

0 to 4/32 to 40

# INDEX